WALK

LAKEL

Butterme ————— west

Paul Hannon

HILLSIDE

HILLSIDE GUIDES - ACROSS THE NORTH

Long Distance Walks
•COAST TO COAST WALK •DALES WAY •CLEVELAND WAY
•WESTMORLAND WAY •FURNESS WAY •CUMBERLAND WAY
•LADY ANNE'S WAY •PENDLE WAY •NORTH BOWLAND TRAVERSE

Hillwalking - Lake District
•LAKELAND FELLS - SOUTH •LAKELAND FELLS - EAST
•LAKELAND FELLS - NORTH •LAKELAND FELLS - WEST

Circular Walks - Peak District
•NORTHERN PEAK •EASTERN PEAK •CENTRAL PEAK
• SOUTHERN PEAK • WESTERN PEAK

Circular Walks - Yorkshire Dales
•HOWGILL FELLS •THREE PEAKS •MALHAMDALE
•WHARFEDALE •NIDDERDALE •WENSLEYDALE •SWALEDALE

Circular Walks - North York Moors
•WESTERN MOORS •SOUTHERN MOORS •NORTHERN MOORS

Circular Walks - South Pennines
•BRONTE COUNTRY •CALDERDALE •ILKLEY MOOR

Circular Walks - Lancashire
•BOWLAND •PENDLE & THE RIBBLE • WEST PENNINE MOORS

Circular Walks - North Pennines
•TEESDALE •EDEN VALLEY

Yorkshire Pub Walks
•HARROGATE/WHARFE VALLEY •HAWORTH/AIRE VALLEY

Large format colour hardback

FREEDOM OF THE DALES

BIKING COUNTRY
•YORKSHIRE DALES CYCLE WAY •WEST YORKSHIRE CYCLE WAY
•MOUNTAIN BIKING - WEST & SOUTH YORKSHIRE
•AIRE VALLEY BIKING GUIDE •CALDERDALE BIKING GUIDE
•GLASGOW Clyde Valley & Loch Lomond

•YORK WALKS City Theme Walks

•WALKING COUNTRY TRIVIA QUIZ Over 1000 questions

Send for a detailed current catalogue and pricelist

WALKING COUNTRY

LAKELAND FELLS
Buttermere & the West

Paul Hannon

HILLSIDE

HILLSIDE
PUBLICATIONS
11 Nessfield Grove
Keighley
West Yorkshire
BD22 6NU

First published 1998

© Paul Hannon 1998

ISBN 1 870141 63 6

*Cover illustrations: Buttermere Valley from Fleetwith Pike;
Pillar Rock from Robinson's Cairn
Back cover: Wastwater Screes from Middle Fell
(Paul Hannon/Big Country Picture Library)*

*Page 1: The Scafells from Middle Fell
Page 3: Yewbarrow from Wastwater*

Printed in Great Britain by
Carnmor Print & Design
95-97 London Road
Preston
Lancashire
PR1 4BA

CONTENTS

INTRODUCTION

The fells of the Lake District are the most impressive and most popular in England. The majority of the National Park's 866 square miles is dominated by its hills, from the rocky fastnesses of Scafell Pike, the summit of England, down to some delightful low-level fells. To do justice to this unique landscape, 100 outstanding fellwalks have been devised and shared among a series of four definitive guidebooks. Together these embrace the best fellwalking in the country, and each guide deals with a logically defined area of Lakeland.

The walks within this volume cover the western part of the National Park, with Buttermere as the focal point. Other popular bases are Wasdale and Eskdale, and some of the best known fells include Scafell, Haystacks, Great Gable and High Stile. The three companion guides feature Ambleside & the South; Patterdale & the East; and Keswick & the North.

Although any number of more demanding walks can be planned by enthusiasts, the aim of this series is to provide a varied range of outings within the scope of most walkers. Thus a limit of around 10 miles and 3500 feet of ascent per walk has been set: most walks are in fact well within these bounds. A feature of these walks is their variety, so that ridgewalks alternate with valley approaches, there are steep climbs, gentle climbs, routes that include mountain tarns and waterfalls. All share the character that makes the Lakeland Fells so special.

The great majority of the Lakeland Fells is freely open to walkers, though many of the routes described are in any case on public rights of way. Any access routes onto the hills are always on rights of way or permitted routes. Please be sensitive when passing near farms and dwellings, and if you must take a dog with you, ensure it is on a lead. While we may have every right to be there, the sheer weight of our numbers means it is particularly important to also act responsibly.

Mountain safety is a subject dealt with in several chunky volumes, and here it should be sufficient to say that the most important elements are to be properly equipped, and realistically aware of the three great limitations of time, physical condition and weather. An ability to use map and compass is strongly recommended, as one can be easily disorientated in mist. In winter conditions the fells take on an entirely different character. In such circumstances even the humblest of fells present new dangers: ice, snow, bitterly cold or gale force winds, and

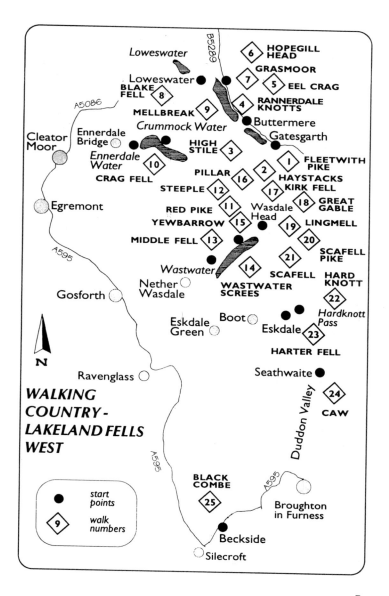

Loweswater

HOPEGILL HEAD ⟨6⟩

GRASMOOR ⟨7⟩

⟨5⟩ EEL CRAG

Loweswater

BLAKE FELL ⟨8⟩

⟨4⟩ RANNERDALE KNOTTS

MELLBREAK ⟨9⟩

Crummock Water

Buttermere

Gatesgarth

Cleator Moor

Ennerdale Bridge

HIGH STILE ⟨3⟩

⟨1⟩ FLEETWITH PIKE

Ennerdale Water

⟨10⟩

⟨2⟩

CRAG FELL

PILLAR ⟨16⟩

HAYSTACKS

Egremont

STEEPLE ⟨12⟩

⟨17⟩ KIRK FELL

RED PIKE ⟨11⟩

Wasdale Head

⟨18⟩ GREAT GABLE

YEWBARROW ⟨15⟩

⟨19⟩ LINGMELL

MIDDLE FELL ⟨13⟩

⟨20⟩

Wastwater

⟨21⟩ SCAFELL PIKE

⟨14⟩

Nether Wasdale

SCAFELL

WASTWATER SCREES

HARD KNOTT

Gosforth

⟨22⟩

Boot

Hardknott Pass

Eskdale Green

Eskdale ⟨23⟩

HARTER FELL

Ravenglass

Seathwaite

WALKING COUNTRY - LAKELAND FELLS WEST

Duddon Valley

⟨24⟩ CAW

● start points

⟨9⟩ walk numbers

BLACK COMBE ⟨25⟩

Broughton in Furness

Beckside

Silecroft

N

A5086
A595
B5289
A5095

short daylight hours all demand greater preparation. In true winter conditions one should carry ice axe and crampons and be competent in their use. Don't be put off the winter experience, however, for it is in this season that the fells are seen at their most stunningly beautiful.

The overwhelming popularity of these hills is all too evident to those who set foot upon them. Many paths are worn wide and bare, and in most parts of the district evidence of repair work will be encountered. In recent years this has grown into a major undertaking, with the National Park and the National Trust at the forefront. In most cases the paths are sensitively restored with stone surfaces, a dramatic improvement on the ugly scars they replace. Wherever possible please adhere to the paths old and new, and to any diversions during ongoing pathwork. Additionally, walkers can show respect for our fragile hills by faithfully following zigzags and avoiding insensitive short-cuts; not descending at speed; not walking the fells in enormous groups; and by wearing the lightest footwear that doesn't jeopardise safety.

Most of the walks begin from villages or recognised parking areas, but please be sure not to obstruct local access. Many walks can also be accessed by public transport, so even if you came to the district by car, consider the local bus whenever possible in order not to exacerbate peak season traffic congestion. Stagecoach Cumberland produces an annual timetable which includes numerous seasonal services.

Using the guide
Each walk is self-contained, featuring essential details, sketch map, and route description including comment on features along the way. The basic maps serve merely to identify the location of the routes, for which a 1:25,000 scale map is strongly recommended. Best known for their excellent detail are the Ordnance Survey Outdoor Leisure maps, of which four cover the Lake District (1998 editions onward):-

    4 - English Lakes North West   5 - English Lakes North East
    6 - English Lakes South West   7 - English Lakes South East
(all walks in this guide are on sheets 4 and 6)

Useful for general planning purposes are the Landranger maps at 1:50,000, and two sheets covers the area:
        89 - West Cumbria; 96 - Barrow in Furness & South Lakeland

The increasingly popular Harvey Maps also cover the district, and their 1:25,000 scale Superwalker maps are available as follows:
North West Lakeland   Western Lakeland   Northern Lakeland
Eastern Lakeland   Southern Lakeland   Central Lakeland

SOME USEFUL ADDRESSES

Ramblers' Association 1/5 Wandsworth Road, London SW8 2XX
Tel. 0171-339 8500

Lake District National Park Visitor Centre
Brockhole, Windermere (on A591)   Tel. 015394-46601

National Park/Tourist Information

Town Hall, Market Street, **Cockermouth**	Tel. 01900-822634
Market Hall, Market Place, **Whitehaven**	Tel. 01946-695678
Moot Hall, Market Square, **Keswick**	Tel. 017687-72645
Seatoller Barn, **Seatoller**	Tel. 017687-77294
The Square, **Broughton-in-Furness**	Tel. 01229-716115

Public Transport
Cumbria Journey Planner - Tel. 01228-606000
National Rail Enquiries - Tel. 0345-484950

Lake District Weather - Tel. 017687-75757

Lake District National Park Authority
Murley Moss, Oxenholme Rd, Kendal LA9 7RL Tel. 01539-724555

Cumbria Tourist Board
Ashleigh, Holly Road, Windermere LA23 2AQ   Tel. 015394-44444

Friends of the Lake District
No.3, Yard 77, Highgate, Kendal LA9 4ED   Tel. 01539-720788

The National Trust North West Regional Office
The Hollens, Grasmere, Ambleside LA22 9QZ   Tel. 015394-35599

The Country Code
- Respect the life and work of the countryside
- Protect wildlife, plants and trees
- Keep to public paths across farmland
- Safeguard water supplies
- Go carefully on country roads
- Keep dogs under control • Guard against all risks of fire
- Fasten all gates • Leave no litter - take it with you
- Make no unnecessary noise
- Leave livestock, crops and machinery alone
- Use gates and stiles to cross fences, hedges and walls

SUMMITS	
FLEETWITH PIKE	2126ft/648m
HONISTER CRAG	2077ft/633m

START Gatesgarth   **Grid ref.** NY 194149

DISTANCE 4 miles/6½km   **ASCENT** 1800ft/548m

ORDNANCE SURVEY MAPS
1:50,000 - Landranger 89 **or** 90   1:25,000 - Outdoor Leisure 4

ACCESS Start from the roadside car park opposite the farm, on the B5289 between Buttermere and the Honister Pass. Seasonal daily bus service from Keswick (circular via Buttermere and Borrowdale).

At the head of Buttermere's lovely sheet of water rises the familiar outline of Fleetwith Pike, a mountain that hides little, and offers its west ridge as a delectable staircase to the summit.

S From the car park a short stroll along the road leads to the open fell below Fleetwith Pike. Ignoring the broad track heading right, the Fleetwith path soon materialises to commence an immediate assault on the very foot of the ridge, directly ahead. At this point most of the impending ascent is clearly in view. The climb's popularity has resulted in a restored zigzag section up past a century-old white memorial cross before slanting up onto the crest of the ridge. A grassy interlude is soon eclipsed as Fleetwith Edge takes shape in the heather.

The walking improves throughout, the main difficulty being to remember to stand still to absorb the unfolding panorama as old favourites such as Pillar, Grasmoor and Great Gable enter the scene at various stages. An unchanging aspect of this stairway to heaven is the retrospective view of the Buttermere Valley, which is quite simply a gem. The miniature rock barriers of the final 500 feet form an inviting ladder to the summit, making this a memorable mile and a truly memorable hour.

Although a good path makes a direct slant down to Dubs Quarry, visible to the south-east, a more interesting return conducts a little exploration of Fleetwith's hinterland. From the cairn another path heads east, lesser branches adventurously skirting the tops of the mighty cliffs of Honister Crag. The path runs on past a couple of pools, then over or round a minor knoll to find another pool directly below the dramatically sited peak of Black Star.

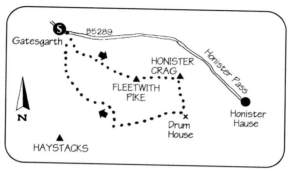

Though the main path and our onward route bears right of the pool and turns south-east to abandon the edge, first take the thinner path across the pool to scale the brief slope onto the neatly cairned top of Black Star. This is the true summit of Honister Crag, the dark shadow which hangs almost vertically above the upper reaches of Honister Pass, with Gatesgarthdale and the narrow strip of tarmac below: riddled with tunnels and tracks from years of quarrying, it is one of Lakeland's grandest cliffs.

Back on the main path, this descends pleasantly on a line for the remains of the Drum House in the broad saddle below. Backed by Grey Knotts, it sits at the highest point of an old tramway linking Honister and Dubs Quarry, and is further identified with Moses' Trod climbing away across Grey Knotts' flank. En route we descend to the extensive former slate workings at Hopper Quarry, with glimpses into Borrowdale down to the left. Follow its access road out to the left, briefly, before a thin path branches off for the final couple of minutes to the ruin of the Drum House. Now utilised as a popular pathway, the old tramway can be followed down to the right to the substantial remains at Dubs, entering the site in style through a cutting in slate walls. En route, Haystacks is seen directly ahead, with mighty Pillar looking preposterously bigger behind!

Ignoring a branch left which drops down to cross the beck in Dubs Bottom, keep straight on past a stone hut maintained as a useful shelter. Beyond the workings the path soon loses height more rapidly as it runs above a colourful ravine occupied by Warnscale Beck, which features some fine waterfalls. On swinging away from the beck, this well engineered former quarry track curves down the lower flanks of Fleetwith Pike into Warnscale Bottom, to then offer a steady amble out onto the road where the walk began.

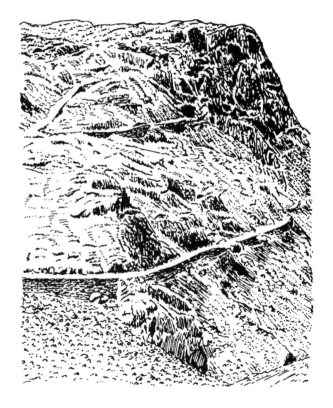

Honister Crag

2 HAYSTACKS

SUMMITS
HAYSTACKS   1958ft/597m

START *Gatesgarth*   **Grid ref.** *NY 194149*

DISTANCE *4½ miles/7km*   **ASCENT** *1700ft/518m*

ORDNANCE SURVEY MAPS
1:50,000 - Landranger 89 or 90   1:25,000 - Outdoor Leisure 4

ACCESS *Start from the roadside car park opposite the farm, on the B5289 between Buttermere and the Honister Pass. Seasonal daily bus service from Keswick (circular via Buttermere and Borrowdale).*

Haystacks is a justly popular, if unkempt chunk of heaven. Traversing the fell from end to end, this leisurely exploration opens up a veritable box of delights, with silvery tarns and craggy tors scattered around the heather, and views of stunning quality.

S From the car park take the path between the farm buildings, and while crossing the fields beyond, there is ample time to appraise the walk's objective ahead to the left. Haystacks may be surrounded by higher mountains, but it is far from dominated by them. On crossing the bridge over Warnscale Beck, those first easy minutes are soon forgotten as the climb begins in earnest. An initially steep section is eased with the aid of zigzags around a small plantation.

Any halts for respite will earn glorious views back over the Buttermere Valley, while Fleetwith Pike is a permanent fixture across Warnscale Bottom. Higher up, the gradients ease and the well worn path slants half-left across the lower flanks of High Crag to gain the green hollow of Scarth Gap. At 1425ft/434m this is one of the district's lower foot passes, but its setting is as impressive as any. Revealed ahead are Great Gable and Kirk Fell, quickly joined by mighty Pillar. A cairn and, bizarrely, a surviving gate from the Ennerdale watershed fence occupy the highest point.

To the left the final 500 feet of Haystacks await, and a few yards from the cairn the climb recommences. Crummock Water soon joins Buttermere in the retrospective view, well ahead of Ennerdale Water's appearance. The path rises unfailingly and enjoyably, numerous rebuilt sections linking with natural mini-clambers. Shortly after savouring a splendid prospect of the rock tower of Big Stack above Warnscale Bottom, the summit is reached in style. The fell's character is encapsulated in its highest ground, where two solid cairns of equal standing crown a short rocky ridge, beneath which the waters of a surprisingly extensive tarn lap a rocky shoreline. Major features of the view include the great wall of Pillar across the head of lonely Ennerdale, so often brooding in shadow; and Great Gable's unmistakeable dome at that valley's head, dwarfing its satellite Green Gable. The Buttermere Valley presents the most attractive scene, stretching away between the mountain walls of High Crag on the left and the delectable Grasmoor group to the right.

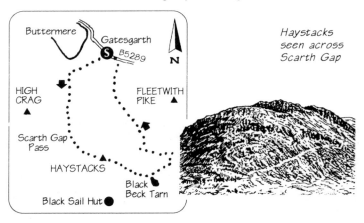

*Haystacks
seen across
Scarth Gap*

From the southernmost cairn on the ridge, the return path sets forth eastwards across the broad and entirely absorbing main ridge of the fell. The first target is Innominate Tarn, nestling amid heathery knolls and glistening prominently from the summit cairn. Many years before his demise, Wainwright selected the shores of this lovely pool for the scattering of his ashes - the master guidebook writer was always a shrewd judge of a grand setting. Beyond here the path drops down through inspiring surroundings to cross the outflow of Black Beck Tarn, which is fully revealed on the short climb beyond. Ignoring any lesser branches, the path passes around the back of Green Crag before a steady descent towards Dubs Bottom. Across the other side, on the slopes of Fleetwith Pike, are the conspicuous remains of Dubs Quarry.

Set back up to our right is the fine 'island' crag of Great Round How, and a little after a path from there merges into ours, it is time to leave the main highway. A large cairn marks the start of a path branching left, just before the main path drops down to pass beneath the prominent tilted slab of Little Round How. This cairned path descends past a less obtrusive quarry site, though on approaching Warnscale Beck, an easy mistake is to take a branch continuing straight down to cross it immediately above a deep ravine, joining the bridleway opposite. However, a couple of adjacent cairns send our intended path branching left, keeping well above the ravine and enjoying better views into the splendid waterfall.

The path slants interestingly down as it takes advantage of a former quarrymans' way. This descends above the ravine then zigzags expertly down below Haystacks' menacing cliffs into the sanctuary of Warnscale Bottom, where a footbridge crosses the beck to join the bridleway that is the old quarry track from Dubs. The return to Gatesgarth is completed in fine style on a luxuriant green path through the bracken. On meeting the Honister road the farm is only a few yards down to the left.

North-west from Haystacks: the Grasmoor fells rise out of a mist-choked Buttermere Valley

```
              SUMMITS
   HIGH STILE   2648ft/807m
   RED PIKE     2477ft/755m
```

START Buttermere   **Grid ref.** NY 175169

DISTANCE 6½ miles/10½km **ASCENT** 2477ft/755m

ORDNANCE SURVEY MAPS
1:50,000 - Landranger 89   1:25,000 - Outdoor Leisure 4

ACCESS *Start from the village centre, there are two car parks (the National Trust one is on the Cockermouth road). Summer bus service from Keswick (via Whinlatter and Borrowdale).*

A hugely satisfying direct assault on one of Lakeland's favourite sons, a pleasurable adventure which involves scaling the impending northeast ridge. The views are excellent throughout, and the climb itself is less demanding than anticipated.

❺ From Buttermere a wealth of delightful paths radiate, and most popular is the fenced track that runs to the left of the *Fish Hotel* and along to the foot of the lake. Buttermere itself is in view from the outset, while up ahead Sourmilk Gill tumbles through the trees, and High Stile waits high on the skyline. Crossing both the outflow and Sourmilk Gill, a path heads left along the shore. After just 100 yards take a branch slanting up to the right, to gain some easy height within Burtness Wood. About 100 yards beyond a parallel wall and beck, a thin green trod heads off to the right, soon leaving the wood at a stile. At once the views open out over Buttermere to the Dale Head group, and more impressively Fleetwith Pike.

This super little path heads along to the left, just sufficiently evident to be followed in its near level course. As a wall comes in for company, it gradually rises more determinedly and more clearly as a green way through the bracken to approach Burtness Comb. Up above, High Crag thrusts forward a massive buttress, to be quickly joined by the crags overlooking the peaceful hollow of Burtness Comb. On parting company with the wall, the main path swings up to the right rather than entering the amphitheatre of the comb, setting its sights firmly on the currently ill-defined north-east ridge of High Stile. It can be seen as a scarred stony section just above, though happily this proves to be a brief disruption of an otherwise splendid route.

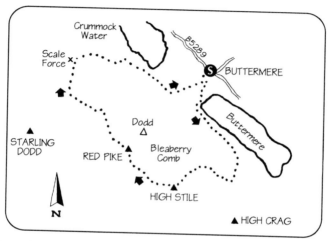

The path quickly swings off right again, winding a grand course at an undemanding gradient: working more to the Buttermere side of the ridge, the lake is joined by Crummock Water, with the Grasmoor fells grouped behind the village. Climbing through heather a rib of modest outcrops neatly delineate the edge of the curving ridge, and though nowhere remotely precarious, it provides an excellent route to the summit. A good moment is experienced as Red Pike is revealed across Bleaberry Comb, with Bleaberry Tarn quickly appearing on the floor of this hanging valley. The uppermost section offers a final boss of rock which proves the gateway to the extensive top. By now Great Gable, the Scafells and Pillar are arrayed over the ridge out to High Crag. As the path falters keep left a little further to look down over the crags of Burtness Comb before moving onto the centrally sited summit cairn.

High Stile is the central and loftiest peak on the high ridge separating Buttermere from Ennerdale, and makes a classic mountain study: steep, untrodden slopes fall south to the Ennerdale plantations, and arms branch east and west to the two outstanding supporting tops of High Crag and Red Pike. To the north a rim of crags overlook two combs, while in between, a formidable buttress projects high above Buttermere, this jewel of a lake lapping the wooded base of the mountain. The felltop is uncharacteristically broad, while remaining rough and stony. One of Lakeland's finest viewpoints is greatly enhanced by witnessing the sensational plunges into the two combs which add great depth to pictures of Buttermere and Fleetwith Pike, and Crummock Water and Grasmoor respectively.

A line of cairns points the way to merge with old fenceposts bound for the western edge of High Stile's top, crowned by a cairn on a boss of rock. This proves a first class vantage point, with Bleaberry Tarn in its comb far below, and Red Pike pushing elegantly skyward. This splendid top is the next objective on the march of the great High Stile ridge, with a good path linking the two mountains. A short, stony descent leads quickly down to an impressive stance at the head of Chapel Crags Gully. A short grassy stroll then precedes the gentlest of rises, swinging right, and briefly faintly, up onto Red Pike's small top.

Of the many grand fells ranged above Buttermere, this shapely peak sited directly opposite the village claims greatest affinity. Its top juts out with prominence from the ridge, but the severity of the mountain's face is such that the summit is out of sight from the village centre. This is a well defined perch, exposed and barren with a sprawl of stones that struggle to succeed as either cairn or shelter. The same rich colour as the dusty path descending to Bleaberry Tarn, there is no doubt as to how this fell came by its name. Two classic features of the panorama are the aerial view of the tarn backed by High Stile, and the more complete picture of Crummock Water and the scree-draped Grasmoor fells. The inclusion of Buttermere, Loweswater, Ennerdale Water and Derwentwater makes this one of the best 'Lakes' viewpoints.

Descent begins instantly, heading north-west on a zigzag path down easy screes to the start of Lingcomb Edge. As a branch goes off left on the watershed towards the grassy dome of Starling Dodd, simply keep to the well defined edge path, with Crummock Water looking grand beyond the hollow of Ling Comb. On reaching the heather zone, a broad path branches left off the edge, and though initially doubling back, it quickly makes a broad descent to little Scale Beck. Turning downstream it takes in an attractive if rather confined section which can be sticky on a hot day.

Just after a stony path merges in from above we drop down a little slab, to then have a choice of routes down to Scale Force. Either side of the beck supports paths as the stream enters a wooded ravine in readiness for its moment of glory. The left branch is gentler, crossing the beck and escaping its confines before a short spiral down to the bridge at the foot of Scale Force; the more popular right branch stays closer to the beck, having been partly rebuilt as it drops down to the same point. The shy waterfall makes an impressive sight if venturing the few yards nearer to gain a better glimpse into its secretive ravine.

Beyond Scale Force the path heads off through a gateway, traversing the fellside as it wisely keeps well above marshy terrain near the head of Crummock Water. Eventually however it suddenly drops down nearer the lake, an unclear moment aided by a couple of useful pointer cairns. The path recommences at a lower level, with Buttermere ahead now, and Red Pike returning high above us. Without ever reaching the shore the path runs beneath the woods above the alluvial plain between Crummock Water and Buttermere, and accompanies the linking Buttermere Dubs up towards the latter. Midway along it is spanned by the stone-arched Scale Bridge, and by crossing it the walk ends in the way it began, along a fenced lane back into the village.

The head of Buttermere from High Stile, looking to Robinson, Hindscarth, Dale Head and Fleetwith Pike

```
                    SUMMITS
RANNERDALE KNOTTS    1165ft/355m
```

START Crummock Water   **Grid ref.** NY 162193

DISTANCE 3½ miles/5½km   **ASCENT** 820ft/250m

ORDNANCE SURVEY MAPS
1:50,000 - Landranger 89   1:25,000 - Outdoor Leisure 4

ACCESS *Start from the first parking area on Cinderdale Common, after the B5289 by the lake breaks out onto the base of the open fell beyond Rannerdale Farm. Seasonal daily bus service from Keswick.*

The miniature fell of Rannerdale Knotts looms large and aggressively over the two settlements of Rannerdale, and offers riches beyond compare to any poor soul finding himself in Buttermere with only an hour or two to spare.

S Return along the enclosed road past the dwellings, a short stroll during which Rannerdale Knotts is upstaged by Whiteless Pike behind it, and the graceful Red Pike across the lake. When the road opens out again by a short section of lakeshore, leave the road by the first of two adjacent green paths. Adopting an early upper rougher section, this runs on to a saddle at a marshy spring. Here turn left up a broad green way in a slight bowl, climbing steeply to a knoll for what will be an essential break. This offers a stunning Buttermere prospect, with the lake enclosed in its deep bowl by Fleetwith Pike and Haystacks.

The wispish path doubles back here, climbing steeply through gorse to emerge onto easier ground. Almost the whole of Crummock Water is below by now, with Loweswater behind, and on a clear day the Galloway Hills across the sea. Bearing left the climb resumes, soon easing out on the ridge-end. The immediate neighbours of Grasmoor and Whiteless Pike are revealed in front. The path rises right to quickly gain the felltop, marked by a cairn on this summit of miniature tors.

Rannerdale Knotts provides indisputable evidence that the best views come neither from mountain tops nor valleys, but from points in between. From the brash wall of Grasmoor to the dalehead bowl of fells, the panorama belongs exclusively to the Buttermere Valley. Buttermere's still waters are barely discernible when reflecting the bowl of famous mountains they fill, while by striding a few yards out to the ridge-end two vast sections of Crummock Water merge at one's very feet. Beyond, unsung Loweswater confirms this as the best viewpoint for the triumvirate of lakes.

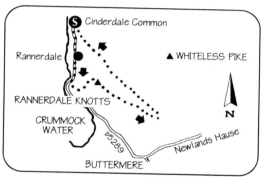

Leave by the broad path heading east along the ridge of Low Bank, and ensure this gently declining stroll is taken slowly to fully absorb the glories all around: the Buttermere scene is incomparable. Ultimately the ridge terminates at the Rannerdale col, a path junction where our fell is linked to Whiteless Pike, whose ascent path beckons (see WALK 5). Instead however, double sharply back to the left, on another green path ambling down the secluded side valley of Rannerdale. Grasmoor and Whiteless Pike quickly return to the view. It is difficult to imagine that this 'hidden' valley witnessed a battle many centuries ago, when Norman forces were surprised by a band of local men.

The path runs gently down along the base of Rannerdale Knotts to reach a gate in the wall junction at the bottom corner. Through it a footbridge crosses Squat Beck and the path merges into another green way. Bear left on this, running out of the valley on this broad green track. Splendid views are enjoyed over the farming pastures and the lake to Mellbreak, while above us, Whiteless Pike returns to its graceful best: a grand finale. The path leads unfailingly back to the start on Cinderdale Common.

```
          SUMMITS
WHITELESS PIKE   2165ft/660m
  WANDOPE   2533ft/772m
  EEL CRAG   2753ft/839m
    SAIL   2536ft/773m
```

START Buttermere   **Grid ref.** NY 175169

DISTANCE 6½ miles/10½km **ASCENT** 2706ft/825m

ORDNANCE SURVEY MAPS
1:50,000 - Landranger 89 **or** 90   1:25,000 - Outdoor Leisure 4

ACCESS Start from the village centre. There are two car parks. Seasonal bus service from Keswick (via Lorton or Borrowdale).

A magnificent outing on airy ridges typical of the Grasmoor fells.

S From the road bridge in front of the *Bridge Hotel*, a kissing-gate sends a path through Ghyll Wood above Sail Beck. Towards the end of the trees, a ladder-stile accesses the open fell. Take the path rising directly through bracken to a path crossroads. Go left for two minutes to a level crossroads, then double back right to climb to a knoll. Already there are big views back over Buttermere to High Stile, Haystacks and Great Gable; Crummock Water soon appears too. Whiteless Pike appears ahead before the path runs on to a cairn at the Rannerdale col, with Loweswater and the coast now appearing. This junction of ways sends branches left along Rannerdale Knotts and also down its side valley. Now the ascent gets down to business, a zigzag preceding a climb that eases out around the shoulder of Whiteless Breast. The ever extending views back are dominated by the High Stile ridge, with Sourmilk Gill tumbling down beneath Red Pike.

As the upper section of our fell appears ahead, a gentle amble sees Causey Pike make a splendid entrance through the Rigg Pass, along with most of the route in fact. The path recommences a steep pull to some interesting tilted slabs, above which pleasant climbing leads to the neat summit. Some will see Whiteless Pike only as a passport to loftier fare, but here there is unlikely to be a desperate urge to move on, and certainly this is a worthy objective in its own right. Small in extent, the summit exudes a sense of airiness - there's a lot more sky than earth in the vicinity! As a viewpoint it is well favoured, the brash front of Grasmoor lurking menacingly behind, and the manifold delights of the Buttermere Valley very firmly to the fore.

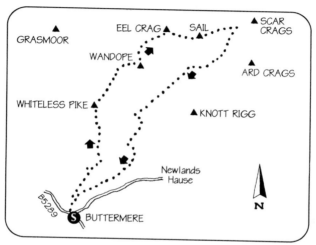

Resume north along the only possible option, enjoying a brief descent to the col of Saddle Gate before an equally pleasant pull up Whiteless Edge onto Thirdgill Head Man, a useful marker cairn at the very top of the slope (the path passes just below it to the east). From here strike out north-east, and a thin path forms on the moor-like Wandope Moss to rise gently to the tiny cairn on Wandope. This is found to hover a mere stride from a very steep fall into Addacomb Hole, a stunning example of a hanging valley whose walls plunge dramatically from the edge. The distant panorama is also meritorious, the finest aspect being the mountain grouping in the heart of the district.

Wandope is linked to Eel Crag by a fine walk around the top of Addacomb Hole. A path skirts the rim of this combe, clinging tight on the ascent before rising left to gain Eel Crag's summit. An Ordnance

Survey column crowns the highest point of the bare, slaty top on which paths have made little impression. Often referred to as Crag Hill, this second summit in the Grasmoor group shakes off its 'bridesmaid' tag with the aid of greater geographical superiority. Eel Crag's pivotal role makes it kingpin of the fells south of Coledale Hause, yet is the only major top in the group without a valley foothold.

Craggy slopes line the north-east and south edges of the plateau, though with care, in mist, they also act as infallible guides to the commencement of the only possible line of descent in this direction. The way off is indicated by a cairn south-east of the OS column, a good path adhering to the narrow ridge which wastes no time in losing height. On encountering exposed rock hands may be required to do a steadying job, but this adds to the interest rather than to any perils.

The rounded top of Sail is gained beyond a minor col, though its summit cairn stands to the left of the path and is invariably bypassed. Certainly this apologetic pile of stones need not be approached to enhance the view, an excellent mountain panorama from Skiddaw through the heart of the district to the western fells. Nature made Sail a high-altitude stepping stone by placing it on one of Lakeland's most popular ridges, and few will see it as anything more.

From Sail this high ridge takes another step nearer the valley by falling to Sail Pass. The broad path descending thereto is rather dull after the drop off Eel Crag, but uninterrupted views over Newlands and the Vale of Keswick amply compensate. At the well defined junction of ways take the clear path doubling back to the right. This vacates the ridge by slanting very pleasantly through Sail's heather flank down towards Rigg Pass, which links the Ard Crags ridge with this main higher ridge. Though a path runs through it, our path does not drop to join it in the true saddle, but continues further around the flank before a steeper drop left onto it.

The path can be seen ahead as it contours the flanks of our outward fells. Firstly it slants in to cross the tumbling Addacomb Beck beneath the outflow of Addacomb Hole, then commences an even gentler return as it steadfastly refuses to lose height. Just sit back and enjoy the prospect ahead to Sourmilk Gill beneath High Stile and Red Pike. Two beck crossings are encountered, and at each the path shadows the far bank down a short way before resuming across the fell. Ultimately the path slants down to a broader green one below, by the intake wall/fence, running on to rejoin the outward route just above the village.

SUMMITS	
WHITESIDE	2359ft/719m
HOPEGILL HEAD	2526ft/770m
LADYSIDE PIKE	2306ft/703m

START Crummock Water   **Grid ref.** NY 159207

DISTANCE 7 miles/11km   **ASCENT** 2296ft/700m

ORDNANCE SURVEY MAPS
1:50,000 - Landranger 89   1:25,000 - Outdoor Leisure 4

ACCESS Start from Lanthwaite Green at the northern end of Crummock Water, where the B5289 from the Vale of Lorton emerges onto the open fell. There is a car park by the phone box. Seasonal daily bus service from Keswick (circular via Lorton and Borrowdale).

An elegant ridgewalk based on Hopegill Head, whose stature is evidenced by paths approaching from all points of the compass, merging only at its zenith. The two main routes each incorporate a notable supporting top.

S From the car park two great mountains brood over the common. Grasmoor is the forbidding one on the right, and Whiteside the more inviting to the left, fronted by the prominent alp of Whin Ben. Cross the base of Grasmoor towards Whiteside, a path forming to lead to a footbridge on the stream dividing them. This is Liza Beck, emerging from the ravine of Gasgale Gill. Faced with a steep slope the path runs left, then doubles back up the bank above the gill. A clearer path quickly forms to set about a thoroughly splendid climb.

The path steepens to work up through heather onto the plinth of Whin Ben (1355ft/413m), very much a place to break journey. In view since the outset have been the inseparable pairing of Crummock Water and Mellbreak, with Loweswater soon appearing beneath its own fells. Ahead, the upper half of the climb is revealed, while Gasgale Gill drives deep into the fells. An easy rise on grass precedes steeper heather slopes. The crest of a rocky knoll makes only the second obvious halting place of the climb, as the full might of Gasgale Crags is revealed tumbling from the Whiteside ridge, which can now be fully seen leading invitingly along to the peak of Hopegill Head itself.

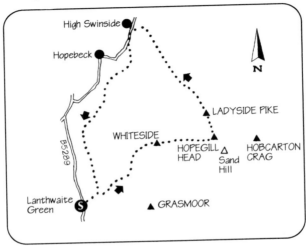

An easy clamber over rougher ground is faced before the going eases, and the cairn on the well defined western top is gained. Very definitely a place to draw breath, such prospects as the Isle of Man and the Vale of Lorton take a back seat to the impending ridgewalk to Hopegill Head, now fully outspread. A further happy thought is that very little climbing remains - for the entire walk. A short stroll leads along to Whiteside's summit, an uncairned top set a few yards off the path. From this crest Gasgale Crags plunge into the ravine of Gasgale Gill, deep-cut gullies forming bold incisions between projecting aretes.

As Hopegill Head's cone beckons, the cragtops can be slavishly followed during this glorious traverse. Though narrow enough to reflect airiness it is unlikely to instil apprehension, and on gaining the modest col, slate increasingly exposes itself underfoot to impart further excitement. The climb to Hopegill Head is rapidly accomplished, incorporating a walk up tilted slabs. The final two minutes are near level, and the summit cannot be missed.

Hopegill Head is a mountain with few faults. The summit epitomises preconceived images of mountain form, with two aretes homing in on it, a massive crag falling away, and above all a sharply defined peak crowned by an upthrust of slate. Finest new feature is the dramatic prospect of Hobcarton Crag lining the head of the Hobcarton Valley, and leading round to its own top with Grisedale Pike beyond. Also of note are a fine prospect of the two major Scafells, and a cameo of the improbable pimple of Pike o'Stickle slotting in between Sail and Eel Crag. On a clear day views out from the hills are every bit as good, from the Isle of Man, featuring its 2000ft peak Snaefell, around a vast sweep of the Solway Firth backed by the Galloway Hills.

The next move is guaranteed to leave any crowds behind, for no-one else is likely to take the ridge heading north. A clear path descends steeply and quickly to encounter the western limits of Hobcarton Crag, where bare rock adds a hint of mountaineering to this crossing onto Ladyside Pike's waiting summit. A peep through the doorway known as the Notch offers a sobering prospect of the immediate declivity below our route's innocently angled slabs. Hobcarton Crag is a bit special, being less of a sheer face than a series of outcrops knitted together with heather, the splintery Skiddaw slate here seen at its most impressive.

After the Notch the path skirts around a rocky pinnacle which could also be tackled head on, then a minor saddle interrupts the path's amble up onto Ladyside Pike. This third and final summit of the day at last provides a worthwhile cairn, with another, greater one just yards beyond. Most of Lakeland is now hidden behind the impressive pairing of Hobcarton Crag and Hopegill Head, so for the most part it is the views out that will be savoured.

The uncomplicated descent is entirely devoid of the dramas that have gone before. An invigorating march leads down the gentle ridge of Swinside, with regular glances back to see Ladyside Pike tapering to its slender point. Ahead, the delectable Vale of Lorton make a striking contrast to the afforested Hobcarton Valley on the right. The thin path that started out soon fades, which matters little as it is simply a case of shadowing the collapsed wall and/or fence. At the end the now sturdy wall curves left to lead down steeper slopes towards the minor road alongside the farm at High Swinside. The bird's-eye view of Lorton village and its patchwork fields could only be bettered by that of the parascenders who often take flight from this bank.

Towards the bottom a distinct cross-path is encountered, so turn left on this for a contrastingly gentle decline through the bracken. The fading path never quite makes it to the road, but contours on to a point where the road swings away. Here a path is signposted along the base of the fell, with Whiteside up in front. This final stage is an extended level march through the bracken in the company of the intake wall, a delectable stride with lovely views over the Vale of Lorton to the Loweswater Fells. Almost at once the side valley of Hope Beck is encountered by a sheepfold lost in the bracken, an idyllic stream crossing that demands a quality break just as Whin Ben did earlier. Ladyside Pike and Hopegill Head tower at the valley head: it is clear how the latter was so named, though it appears curiously flat-topped from this angle.

The way continues, crossing Cold Gill and on beneath an island pasture, occasionally fainter but with the route always obvious. Grasmoor re-appears ahead and easy strides through the bracken ultimately lead back to the tumbling Liza Beck. This makes a perfect foreground to Grasmoor End as another footbridge leads back over the stream. Strike left across the common to quickly return to the start. En route, the embankment of part of an ancient settlement marked on the map can be seen on the right.

———————————————————— *From WALK 7 opposite*

South-east from Grasmoor: looking over High Snockrigg,
Fleetwith Pike and Haystacks to Gable and the Scafells

> ### SUMMITS
> GRASMOOR   2795ft/852m

START Crummock Water   **Grid ref.** NY 159207

DISTANCE 6 miles/9½km   **ASCENT** 2444ft/745m

ORDNANCE SURVEY MAPS
1:50,000 - Landranger 89   1:25,000 - Outdoor Leisure 4

ACCESS Start from the first parking area on Cinderdale Common, after the B5289 by the lake breaks out onto the base of the open fell beyond Rannerdale Farm. Seasonal daily bus service from Keswick.

An entirely delightful climb with views to match, and a rapid descent featuring a splendid deep-sided ravine.

S From the roadside follow the straight line of Cinderdale Beck upstream. A path slants across to it from the main parking area, crossing it to find a green path rising through the bracken on the east side. Enchanting views feature from the outset, with Grasmoor and Whiteless Pike above, and nearby Rannerdale Knotts backed by High Stile. Regardless of the regular appearance of more and more fells as height is gained, the great saddle of Mellbreak across the expanse of Crummock Water will remain the enduring memory of this ascent.

For some time the path shadows the little beck, enjoying its waterplay before breaking off right as its bank becomes less amenable. The path climbs through steeper bracken onto the lower ridge of Lad Hows: the way becomes more purposeful as heather takes over, helped by a luxuriant spread of bilberry. Loweswater is the next lake to appear, and as the going eases the path rises to the cairn on the flat top of Lad Hows, at 1397ft/426m. Take time to relax on this most obvious halting place of the ascent. Buttermere makes a shy appearance to complete the triumvirate of lakes, while closer to hand across the upper reaches of Rannerdale Beck are Thirdgill Head Man and Whiteless Pike.

Ahead, the upper stage of the climb can also be surveyed, as the ridge curves up onto Grasmoor's skyline. After a few level strides the climb resumes, gentle grass giving way to steeper heather slopes. As the path eases onto Grasmoor's broad top, look down on a fine bird's-eye picture of the Rannerdale scene. The way all but fades as it meets the broad path contouring along the southern edge, and turning left the summit is just a couple of minutes further. The top is occupied by a shapely shelter sited near the southern face.

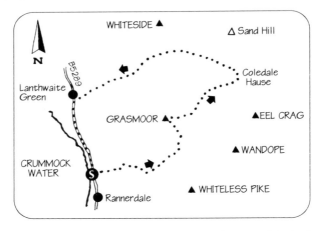

The loftiest mountain between Buttermere and Borrowdale is almost an outlier of the tight-knit massif it crowns: standing aside from busy pedestrian thoroughfares, it is one of the least visited summits of the whole group. In common with many steep-sided mountains, Grasmoor's higher ground is extensive, being a vast plateau ranging a mile from east to west with little decline in altitude. As an all-round viewpoint Grasmoor excels, and from its edges many of Lakeland's mountain groupings are well seen. In addition, it boasts a very extensive sweep of the Solway Firth, backed on a clear day by the Galloway Hills, with the Isle of Man floating in the Irish Sea. Inland are views beyond Lakeland to the Pennine landmarks of Cross Fell, high above the Eden Valley, and Ingleborough, in the Yorkshire Dales.

Besides the described descent, two alternative routes on clear paths take in other fells at little extra effort. These options are Hopegill Head and Whiteside, from Coledale Hause; or Whiteless Pike from the col linking with Eel Crag, finishing down Rannerdale. Certainly in poor conditions, whatever one's objective, it is wiser to return east along the main path, which runs a high level course before descending to the crossroads at the upland depression of the Eel Crag col. Here turn right for Whiteless Pike, or left for Coledale Hause.

For the main route, leave the summit by returning east on the path, but near our joining point veer left, and a slight, cairned line points to the northern edge of the plateau. Here the upper rim of Dove Crags is gained, affording an impressive view over this great amphitheatre and across to the shattered line of Gasgale Crags falling from Whiteside. This surprisingly seldom used route is an obvious line that trades the tedium of the path to the Eel Crag col for this riveting picture of Gasgale Gill and Crags. Trace the cragtops around, and as they fade a clearly defined edge leads a clearer path down towards Coledale Hause, aiming for the shapely Grisedale Pike across the saddle; Coledale itself leads the eye down to the green Vale of Keswick, with the giants of Skiddaw and Blencathra behind.

Only at the very bottom does the path fade, as the stream feeding Gasgale Gill is crossed just yards short of the main Coledale Hause path. A cairn just in front indicates a fork: leave the Coledale descent path in favour of the path remaining with the stream. A little lower, another fork sees a branch run on the 100 yards to the path junction on the true crest of the pass. Ignoring this, again remain with the Gasgale path as it drops down with the lively beck.

So begins a direct and uncomplicated return to the valley, for the deep defile of Gasgale Gill leaves no room for confusion. A good path keeps close tabs on the beck, with a permanent picture of Whiteside's rough wall straight ahead. Surprisingly soon the slopes ease and it is a largely level walk out with the stream. Up to the left Dove Crags on Grasmoor have returned to the scene, and lower down there are varying glimpses out to Mellbreak. After turning a wide corner the portals close in again, briefly, and on emerging the path forks. One can opt to remain with the stream, or take the upper path which contours round to meet the Whiteside ascent path on the slopes of Whin Ben. This then descends to meet the lower path at a simple footbridge on the issuing Liza Beck. From here cross the common beneath Grasmoor End to the phone box by the car park at Lanthwaite Green. Turn left for a gentle stroll back to the start, utilising the broad verges of the open road to enjoy improving views ahead to the High Stile ridge.

SUMMITS

CARLING KNOTT   1784ft/544m
BLAKE FELL   1880ft/573m
GAVEL FELL   1726ft/526m

START Loweswater   **Grid ref.** NY 134210

DISTANCE 6 miles/9½km   **ASCENT** 1886ft/575m

ORDNANCE SURVEY MAPS
1:50,000 - Landranger 89   1:25,000 - Outdoor Leisure 4

ACCESS Start from a National Trust car park at Maggie's Bridge, on a narrow, unsigned cul-de-sac road serving High Nook and Watergate Farms between Loweswater hamlet and lake. Loweswater is served by Buttermere-Ennerdale buses on weekends in high summer.

One of Lakeland's least frequented fells is Blake Fell, loftiest of the tight-knit group of grassy hills collectively known as the Loweswater Fells. It offers rambling off the beaten track in an unspoilt corner.

S From the car park head along the farm road through the fields to Watergate, with Carling Knott thrusting itself forward directly above. The final approach runs within a stone's throw of Loweswater's shore, and a path branches right to a gate into a corner of Holme Wood. Forsake the lakeside path in favour of a slender one climbing through the trees. This settles down to a prolonged, quite steep but pleasant haul up through the wood, changing little in gradient or character.

Ignoring any cross paths and tracks, the way ultimately emerges with delightful views over Loweswater. The path runs on just a little further to a kissing-gate accessing the open fell, and just yards above, a green bridle-track is joined. Though it can be seen far to the right as it swings round the flank of Burnbank Fell, follow it left on a gentle rise back above the wood to where a fence meets the wall. Ahead, Crummock Water makes a splendid appearance.

Through the gate, leave the track and trace the fence up beneath Carling Knott's northerly prow. On reaching the impasse of a small crag, rise above it to find a traversing path. However, beyond the crag leave it in favour of the slopes above, where a natural line suggests itself up slopes of bilberry and scattered stones. The vegetation is less luxuriant towards the top, where a small stone ruin nestles in a hollow beneath a fine cairn on the brow. This abrupt termination of Carling Knott is a better location than the actual summit, which sits back from the action. New views are the order of the day, and though Mellbreak and Honister Crag earn acclaim, the prize goes to the Pillar group.

A faint path forms to rise gently onto the flat top of Carling Knott, which bears several piles of stones, the highest point being occupied by a well built circular shelter. Having failed to merit classification as a 'Wainwright', this minor top is even quieter than its neighbouring fells. Only at this late stage of the climb does Blake Fell reveal itself, now just a steady stroll away. A thin path

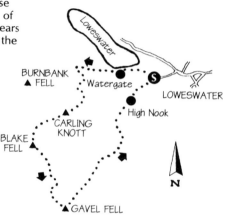

resumes on the miniature scarp on the eastern edge of the ridge, offering a ready made viewing platform for the fell country inland. This runs south-west to a saddle before a simple continuation to a watershed fence. The illogical absence of stiles is a situation which has not improved since lamented by Wainwright as far back as the 1960s! Cross with care at a suitable point: the other side supports both a path and the summit of Blake Fell up to the left.

The oddly sited fence chooses to skirt the top of this shapely hummock bedecked by a sprawling shelter. Attainment of this high point of the Loweswater Fells combines with the dearth of fellow humans and the lushness of the springy turf to encourage one to linger. While the view divides mountains and coast, most eyes will be glued to the hill country where the Pillar, High Stile and Grasmoor groups rise above Ennerdale and Buttermere. Other features of note are an improved picture of Buttermere backed by Fleetwith Pike and Honister Crag; and the distant pairing of Catstycam and Helvellyn. Additionally, there is an extensive panorama out of Lakeland to the Cumbrian coast. Slopes fall away steeply to the south to reveal the very independent cone of Knock Murton above Cogra Moss Reservoir. Currently, our third and final top Gavel Fell appears exceedingly insignificant.

A clear path departs south, rejoining the fence in time to ignore a less usefully placed stile. Descend with the fence, passing the remains of a sheepfold alongside it and down to a fence junction, with Gavel Fell now better appreciated. The right branch curves around the attractive ridge to Knock Murton, but cross the stile and descend the left branch to the saddle of Fothergill Head. The best route crosses the stile in the saddle and heads away for a minute to pick up a curving green track above the well defined head of Comb Gill. Turn left on the track which climbs to a fence corner and continue up onto Gavel Fell's broad top.

The unmarked highest point is crossed by the fence before reaching another fence junction, though the shapely cairn is found 50 yards past the junction on a little mound. It has a good view of the fell's roots in Ennerdale's pastureland, while the mountain scene to the east, featuring in particular Red Pike and Pillar, is given good perspective by an intervening gap of lower country.

Leave by returning to the fence junction and crossing the stile. In poor visibility one can opt to trace the fence heading away, all the way down to meet the bridleway out of Whiteoak Moss. For greater interest, head diagonally away from both fences, dropping to a heathery saddle whose marsh is negotiated by a thin trod to rise onto a pleasant cairned top. This faint way then runs along the broad ridge before faltering at the well defined end above Black Crag.

As the path reforms be sure to bear right to avoid dangerous slopes, then savour an immensely inviting descent of the ridge end, made more rewarding by views of Crummock Water and Loweswater, with the Vale of Lorton heading away. Directly below, the shy Highnook Tarn is seen in its basin at the foot of Carling Knott. As the ridge levels out an old bridleway is met. Go left on this to wind amiably down to a gate off the fell, continuing down to High Nook Farm. Its drive leads away through the fields to Maggie's Bridge.

MELLBREAK

9

SUMMITS
MELLBREAK NORTH TOP   1670ft/509m
MELLBREAK   1679ft/512m

START Loweswater   **Grid ref.** NY 141209

DISTANCE 6½ miles/10½km   **ASCENT** 1600ft/487m

ORDNANCE SURVEY MAPS
1:50,000 - Landranger 89   1:25,000 - Outdoor Leisure 4

ACCESS Start from the Kirkstile Inn in the centre of the hamlet of Loweswater. The only parking is that for patrons of the inn, with room for several cars just across Church Bridge. There is also space for several cars by the phone box at the road junction. Loweswater is served by Buttermere-Ennerdale buses on weekends in high summer.

Though Mellbreak shuns its more discreet Loweswater colleagues in favour of a full frontal display above Crummock Water, this direct ascent from Loweswater of the aggressively exciting gable end is a real gem. From the outset the views are magnificent.

S Leave the junction beneath the pub by the lane below its garden. Mellbreak dominates the scene as the lane crosses Church Bridge on Park Beck. At Kirkgate Farm an unsurfaced lane takes over to rise left, revealing Whiteside and Grasmoor across Crummock Water. This pleasant walled lane leads to the bottom of a plantation missed by the Ordnance Survey. Here leave the track and climb up the break to gain the open fell. Rising away, Loweswater slots into place back over the treetops. The simple grassy path commences what is clearly going to be a Jekyll & Hyde climb, rising through bracken to the foot of a big scree shoot emanating from a rock gateway.

Sanity can be retained by taking advantage of the slaty path raking left, which then turns to rise back, but without regaining the main path. Instead, our path winds up to the left again, circumventing the stony

35

excesses of the rock gateway. We are rewarded with a champagne moment on gaining the airy stance of a projecting spur, looking across a deep gully to a spectacular craggy face. Throughout the climb there are of course excellent retrospective views embracing the circle of modest fells around Loweswater's basin, in addition to the closer and more dramatic scenery above Crummock Water.

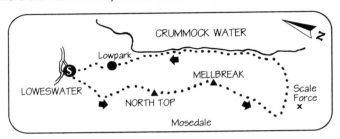

Discerning walkers have formed a thin path up the stony rib, which is scaled enthusiastically to meet the other path above the gateway. The way now spirals up through heather, this upper stage of the ascent being broken at a grassy knoll. This gives a magical view up the valley, as just a few yards to the left a peep reveals Buttermere itself beyond Crummock Water. Before long the going eases for a short stroll to the two scrappy cairns on Mellbreak's North top. Those who have not done their homework will now realise they have not yet climbed Mellbreak, for the true summit is the South top, a long half-mile away and about ten feet higher. A broad, substantial depression separates the two, and thus give the opportunity to remain on high for longer. A path sets off for it, a steady decline keeping to the right side of the saddle and doing a fine job until the halfway point.

As two forks are encountered in quick succession, in each case ignore the right branch. The first is a thinner one slanting down towards Mosedale, but the second is less obvious as a broader path contours straight on Mellbreak's flank: the relevant left branch slants grassily up to regain the broad ridge. It leads steadily up to the summit of the fell, though fading somewhat towards the end. A scrappy cairn on the highest ground is usurped by a creditable one a little to the south, the latter being a useful pointer to the line of descent. While the summit itself offers little obvious interest, the briefest wander in an easterly direction will repay the effort, for the ground falls away to reveal an excessively rough face hurtling down into Crummock Water.

A faint path heads away, crossing and slowly bearing a little to the right of a line of defunct fenceposts. This stride down the grassy southern flank is the easiest way off this side of the fell, and the thin path makes progress even simpler: the views over Crummock Water and up to Buttermere are absolutely magnificent. Aiming for the deep incision of the ravine of Scale Force on the fellside opposite, a minor col is reached before the grassy alp of Scale Knott. The sketchy path passes to its right to drop to a fence, but by bearing half-right over moister ground it will be met nearer a stile at a fence junction. Across the stile, trace the adjoining fence down to a bridle-gate on a cross-path. Turn left on this attractive path above Black Beck, with a view back to the impressive spectacle of the camera-shy waterfall of Scale Force.

Having kept its distance the path drops down to a fence near the confluence with Scale Beck. Passing through a bridle-gate ignore the footbridge and turn downstream towards Crummock Water: a little further, note the divergence of the beck, a rare occurrence! A green path runs through bracken, and just before a sheepfold passes the crumbling walls of an ancient settlement - which in high Summer the bracken effectively conceals - indicated on the Ordnance map.

A little short of the shore is another footbridge. Ignore this too, and break off to the left to gain the lakeside for a prolonged stroll along the base of Mellbreak. The charming peninsula of Low Ling Crag - beneath the more traditional High Ling Crag - makes a tempting halt, a characterful foreground to the cone of Whiteless Pike above Rannerdale Knotts across the lake. Resuming, a succession of brief marshy tracts detract little from the views across to the resplendent Grasmoor group, while Mellbreak's craggy frown is constantly above. Closer to hand, a cluster of gorse bushes form an odd topiary garden.

At a crumbled wall beyond the marshy interludes, a solid wall will be seen some way ahead, and the route makes for its top corner: take the path branching left for a steady rise through bracken well above further quagmires near the foot of the lake. From the wall corner an inviting green path runs along the bottom of a gnarled oakwood, passing above Highpark Farm to a gate at the far corner. Here a leafy old way runs down to the enviable seclusion of the mini-hamlet of Lowpark. Its access road joins a surfaced lane, going left over Park Bridge. A little farther, at another junction, turn left again for a traffic-free return to the pub, enjoying a final prospect of Mellbreak towering as impressively as ever.

```
                    SUMMITS
        CRAG FELL    1715ft/523m
```

START Ennerdale Water   **Grid ref.** NY 085153

DISTANCE 5 miles/8km   **ASCENT** 1400ft/426m

ORDNANCE SURVEY MAPS
1:50,000 - Landranger 89   1:25,000 - Outdoor Leisure 4

ACCESS Start from the Forest Enterprise Broadmoor car park at the foot of the lake. This is reached by taking the Croasdale road out of Ennerdale Bridge, then turning right in half a mile to the road end at the bridge over the lake's outflow. There is a further car park over the bridge. Served by weekend buses from Buttermere in high summer.

Crag Fell's position at the foot of Ennerdale Water is about as isolated as can be in Lakeland. To the average visitor this is just a little too much out of the way, which is wonderful news for the few who do make the effort to seek out the solitude.

S From the plantation cross the bridge over the river Ehen and bear right up past the cottages, on the drive to Crag Farm at the base of the fell. It actually stands at the foot of Grike, a close relative of Crag Fell from which it is divided by the conspicuous ravine of Ben Gill, directly ahead. Before reaching the environs of the farm a wide track branches off to the right, while the true line of the path advances straight on to a stile into the base of the plantation.

Here turn right on a forestry track along the bottom of the plantation, and within 300 yards, just after the wall turns away, a thin path doubles back up to the left. In existence long before the trees were planted, this initially slender way improves into a splendid grassy path, not merely preserved but flourishing as it slants up to leave the plantation behind at a stile. At this point Ennerdale Water appears in fine style below.

Slanting even more gently now, the path runs along to quickly approach the head of Ben Gill's ravine. Here it is but an unassuming stream, but there are splendid views down it, backed by the lakefoot. This is a delectable spot for a break before resuming: ignore the lesser contouring path ahead, and the main path crosses the modest confluence before climbing again. Through colourful vegetation of bracken, heather and bilberry, the path soon rises above a well defined grassy scarp that proves to be an extension of Revelin Crag. The path keeps above the cliffs, and when the going eases the summit is just a short, undulating stroll.

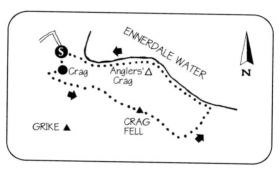

The cairn stands in a surround of grass, oblivious to the characterful face hanging over the lake. Finest feature of the view is the prospect of Ennerdale striking into the heart of the mountains, with many famous peaks displayed from less familiar angles. In favourable weather the next thing to do is step nearer the northern edge to obtain more dramatic views over Ennerdale Water. To commence the return, the now thinner path turns south-east down the grassy flank, aiming towards the saddle with neighbouring but distant Iron Crag, occupied by the upper limits of a plantation on Crag Fell's southern flank.

At a small cairned fork keep left, dropping gently to a stile in the forest fence. Across it, only scattered trees are encountered as the path quickly descends to join a broad grassy track. This is the old road that served the Cragfell Iron Mines, and has since been requisitioned for forestry use. Turn left on it for a very brief stroll to the edge of the trees. Here the fence is met again and the road ends. Passing through the gate, the easiest option is simply to follow the fence down to the right to meet and then follow a sturdy wall descending the fellside. For a minor detour, advance straight on the last vestiges of the mine road, now a slender trod to the modest remains of the mines which appear just ahead: from here contour right, past a small ruined stone hut to meet the descending wall.

Just a little lower, the wall arrives at a junction, immediately above which are a covered shaft and a spoil heap. A stile built into the contouring wall is the key to commencing the descent proper to Ennerdale Water. A thin green path is initially sandwiched between Red Beck and the wall, later breaking out to the other side of the colourful stream as it drops through trees onto the lakeshore path. Immediately on turning left look up to see the spiky Crag Fell Pinnacles thrusting skyward high up the flanks.

As the lakeshore path approaches the landmark of Anglers' Crag, one might apprehensively fear an impasse, such is the way the cliffs plunge enthusiastically into the lapping waters. However a route has been so well worn that only a modest degree of caution is needed to avoid a slip. Beyond this fascinating tangle of scree and rock the path enjoys a delightful final half-mile to leave the base of the fell at the very lakefoot. It crosses a field to the weir at the outflow, where a service road is met to return to the start.

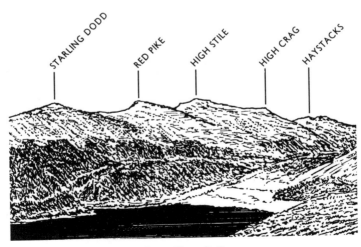

Across Ennerdale Water from Crag Fell

> **SUMMITS**
> *RED PIKE   2710ft/826m*

START *Wastwater*   **Grid ref.** *NY 168068*

DISTANCE *7½ miles/12km*   **ASCENT** *2526ft/770m*

ORDNANCE SURVEY MAPS
1:50,000 - Landranger 89   *1:25,000 - Outdoor Leisure 4 and 6*

ACCESS *Start from the National Trust car park at Overbeck Bridge, by the lakeshore less than two miles south of Wasdale Head.*

An exceptionally easy climb to a magnificent viewpoint: nowhere on this walk are there any gradients of note. Red Pike is an important member of the Wasdale cast of players, exhibiting, above Mosedale, one of the steepest continuous faces in the district. In many valley scenes in Wasdale it hides behind the familiar outline of Yewbarrow, but its most inspiring face can easily be appraised from near the packhorse bridge behind the hotel at Wasdale Head.

S From the car park take the path upstream with Over Beck, to a kissing-gate where the main path turns right, bound for the incredible peak of Yewbarrow. However, through the gate remain on a pleasant green path with the beck. At a stile in an intervening fence the path rises gently above the tree-lined beck. This lively beck scenery makes a softer foreground to the craggy Bell Rib on Yewbarrow, which currently dominates things. Red Pike is also seen up ahead, though for now appears rather tame. On reaching a footbridge opposite the intake wall, cross and turn up by the wall corner.

Rise a short way onto a higher level, contouring path and resume well above Over Beck. Shortly after bridging Brimfull Beck the path begins to fade, and soon attains its nearest acquaintance with Over Beck at a distinctive waterslide. With marshy ground ahead rise left a little before resuming on a faint trod at a slightly higher, drier level. The

41

pronounced saddle of Dore Head is straight ahead, and by now little higher. On levelling out at the marshy basin of Gosforth Crag Moss, a faint trod takes a natural line left to avoid it. Passing beneath craggy slopes rise steadily, now pathless, onto the grassy saddle of Dore Head. This is a fine moment as the peaks encircling Mosedale, including mighty Pillar, simultaneously appear.

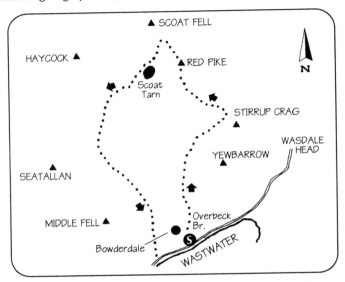

The second half of the climb now begins, the open slopes being a sharp contrast to the albeit lovely restrictions of Over Beck. The gentle nature of the walk belies the amount of climbing involved as the path makes its way effortlessly up the facing slope. A fork is reached below a rash of boulders near the top, the path to the right being a little easier. However, the one clambering through the rocks holds more interest: at the top cairns point the way to the Chair, a rock platform fashioned into a seat with the addition of some of the many stones scattered around. On sitting comfortably one is hit by a bird's-eye view of secretive Low Tarn, while Wastwater itself is of course resplendent beyond. Only a hundred yards further now is the prominent south top, after which the path all but fades for a simple stroll to the summit cairn. For some reason a distinct path from the south top gives the summit a wide berth, opting to contour round to the left.

Although the final yards are a grassy stroll, arrival at the cairn proves no anti-climax, for it is impeccably sited on an airy promontory above the depths of Mosedale. The bold escarpment continues for some distance to both sides, offering ample scope both for inducing vertigo and for filling the viewfinder with the soaring lines of Pillar across the void. Eastwards, the Scafells are well presented above the ridgeline of Yewbarrow, itself dwarfed to the extent that it is almost unnoticed.

Resume along the edge, meeting the by-pass path to arrive within minutes on the saddle linking with Scoat Fell. Turn left down grassy slopes, with Scoat Tarn now fully seen just below. A couple of fenceposts point the way into a grassy hollow. After the stream forms a faint way crosses to drop down the left side to reach the head of the tarn. Tucked hard under Red Pike's ridge, this gem of a tarn is well off the beaten track. From the outflow a thin, clear trod sets off down-stream, with Haycock looming large ahead. A steady descent leads past an old sheepfold complex to a meeting with another stream. Cross the right-hand stream above the confluence to merge with a path from the Haycock-Scoat Fell col.

Resume downstream on what is now a lengthy walk out above Nether Beck. At first Middle Fell and Seatallan dominate ahead, while shortly after rounding a bend the beck enters a foliage-fringed ravine. While some fainter moments now occur on easier ground, the way remains obvious. Towards the bottom the beck enters another ravine with some lovely waterfalls, while Bowderdale Farm appears in its patch-work fields over to the left. As the road appears just below, drop left over part marshy slopes to gain it at a cattle-grid. Turn left over Netherbeck Bridge for the few minutes' walk back to the start.

Red Pike, looking to Scafell

STEEPLE

SUMMITS	
STEEPLE	2686ft/819m
SCOAT FELL	2758ft/841m
HAYCOCK	2614ft/797m

START Ennerdale Water   **Grid ref.** NY 109153

DISTANCE 11 miles/17½km   **ASCENT** 2920ft/890m

ORDNANCE SURVEY MAPS
1:50,000 - Landranger 89   1:25,000 - Outdoor Leisure 4

ACCESS Start from the Forest Enterprise car park at Bowness Knott, east of Ennerdale Bridge. Served by weekend bus from Buttermere in high summer.

A fairly demanding but highly rewarding walk on seldom trodden ways. The ascent of Steeple is the main highlight, and while in truth it is nothing more than a subsidiary top of Scoat Fell, there is a unique individuality that makes Steeple special.

S Head off along the barricaded road in the company of Ennerdale Water, with a fine picture of Crag Fell and Anglers' Crag opposite. After bridging a sidestream an optional path turns off to shadow the lakeshore to its imminent demise. From the head of the lake the path continues a further half-mile with the clear waters of the river Liza to rejoin the road at Irish Bridge. Here cross the Liza and follow the forest road to a gate into the woods. Turn sharp left on the main branch to a similar bridge on Woundell Beck. Just a couple of minutes further a clearing is reached, with a broad track doubling back right, and a broad way rising directly above. Turn up this grassy way, engaging low gear for a steep pull that quickly escapes the trees.

Breaks for respite also earn good views out over Ennerdale Water and across the valley to the duller southern slopes of the High Stile ridge. Though remaining steep, after passing through an old wall a clearer path scales bilberry slopes, and as the last of the trees fade away, the going eases. Rise left to a stile in the fence above, and turn left with the fence leading a grassy way across the heather flanks of Lingmell, under the Tewit How ridge of Scoat Fell.

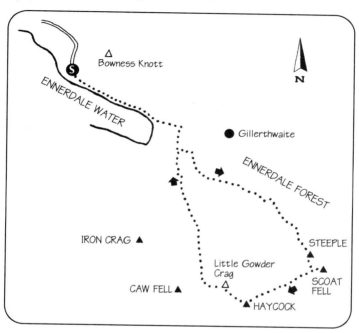

A near-level stride now ensues along this spur, with our ascent line on Steeple revealing itself ahead, and Pillar behind. Beyond a cairned boulder on the brow the fence soon drops away, but the path slants in to the right to cross Low Beck, a worthy place for a break. The ascent path is very clear up the slope ahead, but on heading away the path remains level for a couple of minutes. As it forks take the right branch to set about Steeple's slopes. As the going steepens the occasionally faint path enjoys an increasingly pleasurable climb before easing out on a distinctive knoll. Ahead, the spiky ridge entices even stronger, and it is something of a surprise how easy angled the climb becomes. Successive turrets are gained above increasingly wild scenery, and the climb ends abruptly at the emphatic full-stop of Steeple's summit.

There is room for little else beside the cairn on Steeple's airy top, a place to stand alone, to gaze in awe at nature in the raw: there is nothing pretty here, but there is grandness on a scale seldom experienced in Lakeland. While there are notable drops in all directions, the precipitous plunge into the yawning chasm of Mirk Cove is outstanding - the prospect of Scoat Fell's craggy face and a rarely seen aspect of the full drop of Pillar across the lower Windgap Cove combine to create a scene of total wildness. Respite from the drama can be found in a full-length view of Ennerdale Water down the darkly cloaked valley.

Steeple from Scoat Fell

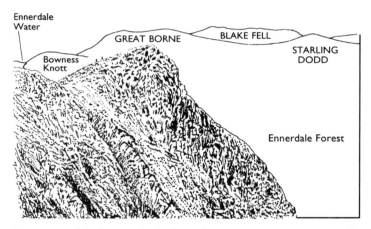

Ennerdale Water

GREAT BORNE   BLAKE FELL

Bowness Knott

STARLING DODD

Ennerdale Forest

Next stage of the journey is the few minutes' crossing onto Scoat Fell, and there is very definitely one route only. The path drops sharply right, down to a saddle where the narrowest section of the walk encounters a short arete during the re-ascent. On the flat top bear left above the headwall of Mirk Cove. Cairns lead to the watershed wall, and the summit is just yards further left. The main cairn is to be found on the other side of one of the gaps, although some bright spark has erected a smaller version on the walltop.

Second only to Pillar in the hierarchy of fells west of Black Sail Pass, Scoat Fell is of far greater significance, geographically, as it stands at a Piccadilly Circus of ridges. Though far from outstanding, Scoat Fell's view has several good and varied aspects, including the dramatic plunge of Red Pike; the sheer immensity of Pillar; and Steeple, inevitably, across Mirk Cove.

Leave by doubling back right with the wall, immediately opening onto grassy terrain with Haycock's distinctive domed top in view ahead. There is little sign of, nor need for, a path as the easiest walking imaginable passes the head of Mirklin Cove (Mirkiln on OS map) during a gentle descent to the saddle below. The trusty wall also leads up the facing slope, a path forming on steeper ground to lead to Haycock's summit.

This stony top is similar to Scoat Fell, and here the wall separates a shelter from a cairn. Few mountains of this altitude are so little known, for Haycock stands on the perimeter of the rough fells. Of the four ridges emanating from Haycock, all but one go on to attain 2000 feet on neighbouring mountains, and in consequence the view from this upland mass lacks intimacy, concentrating instead on a sound if unspectacular all-round panorama.

Once again, depart with the wall, quickly dropping to the rough tor of Little Gowder Crag. What appeared from Haycock as a fine pillar proves to be no more than the wall, seen end-on. Drop off this more cautiously, with a mini scramble down onto a grassy plateau. Ahead along the ridge is the minor top of Caw Fell, but our route now turns for the valley. Slant gently right to a cairn above the start of a broad, unnamed ridge between Silver Cove and Great Cove. Descending past a few minor outcrops and boulders, a thin path quickly forms to lead unfailingly and very pleasantly down this spur bound for Ennerdale.

Several large cairns feature as the path becomes better defined in the heather, with the side valley of Silvercove Beck on the left looking for all the world like a clough on Kinder Scout. Towards the foot of the ridge the path enters a small section of plantation, and a smashing little descent through the trees leads to the very end of the spur. Faced with the confluence and footbridges to either side, take the left one. The path rises onto a bank which it then uses to shadow the newly formed and short-lived Woundell Beck down through the trees. Joining a forest road bear right, and this quickly runs on to the edge of the plantation where the walk entered the trees. From the gate follow the forest road out to Irish Bridge and so back down the valley to the start.

> **SUMMITS**
> *MIDDLE FELL   1909ft/582m*

START *Wastwater*   **Grid ref.** *NY 144056*

DISTANCE *4 miles/6½km*   **ASCENT** *1650ft/503m*

ORDNANCE SURVEY MAPS
1:50,000 - Landranger 89   1:25,000 - Outdoor Leisure 6

ACCESS *Start by Greendale Farm, the first buildings on the Gosforth road branching off the lakeshore road. There are ample parking verges before the road becomes enclosed.*

Middle Fell is a clean-cut package of upland, unashamedly rough and untamed as befits a member of the Wasdale fraternity. Its lack of contour lines on the map ensure the fell remains largely unviolated by booted hordes, and in clear weather this simple fellwalk will be one to remember.

S By the side of the buildings an inviting green path heads for the fell, soon climbing more steeply through bracken. At this early stage the cliffs of Buckbarrow dominate to the left, until, that is, one glances back to see the inimitable Screes already looking majestic across Wastwater. At a distinct corner above Greendale Gill the path forks. That turning in to the gill is the return route, but for now take the easily missed grassy path scaling the foot of the broad ridge to the right.

The path is soon guided by small cairns through a rash of boulders, but then fades to a narrow trod. Keeping more to the stonier ground of the ill-defined ridge on the right, the vague path re-establishes itself, though remains slender throughout the rest of the climb. In clear conditions the use of the path is immaterial on this pleasant climb, which even features a minor scramble near the top. On the summit the path runs a few yards west of the cairn, but this substantial, colourful edifice will take some missing.

The view is occupied entirely by the magnificent Wasdale scene, where every member of this famous cast is keen to get in on the act. Across the sombre waters of the lake, Illgill Head sends down the cliffs, gullies and great fans of the Screes, while to the left the famous grouping of the Scafells overtop all else (see illustration on page 1). Moving around, the unmistakeable cone of Great Gable rules the dalehead, and Kirk Fell peeps over the lower but more interesting Yewbarrow. Further left, the less acclaimed heights of Red Pike, Scoat Fell and Haycock make their own worthwhile contribution.

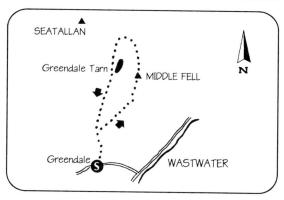

To resume the walk follow the path's sometimes faint course northwards, declining gradually over the broad ridgetop towards the wide saddle with the bulk of loftier Seatallan. A path continues across the col, but here turn down to the left for Greendale Tarn. Marshy terrain above the tarn should be given a wide berth by keeping high above its right (west) bank. On nearing the tarn foot it is safer to turn down to it, where one can accompany either bank of the cheerful stream away. If crossing at the outflow advance a few yards then turn right on an initially faint path, becoming clearer as the beck becomes deeper enclosed. The path on the near bank keeps out of the gill's confines to offer wider views over to Whin Rigg at the foot of Wastwater.

On approaching the twin ravines of Tongues Gills, the grassy tongue of Brown How deflects the thin west bank path down to the beck, to cross Greendale Gill and thus join the other path. The left-hand of these ravines sports a splendid series of vertical falls, perfectly seen from the path. Continuing downstream the path returns in grand style to the outward junction to retrace steps to the road.

SUMMITS
WHIN RIGG 1755ft/535m
ILLGILL HEAD 1998ft/609m

START *Wasdale Head*   **Grid ref.** *NY 182074*

DISTANCE *8½ miles/13½ km*   **ASCENT** *2034ft/620m*

ORDNANCE SURVEY MAPS
1:50,000 - Landranger 89   1:25,000 - Outdoor Leisure 6

ACCESS *Start from the National Trust's Wasdale Head car park by its campsite at the head of Wastwater, 1 mile before the hamlet.*

This walk is a unique experience: many gaze in awe at the Wastwater Screes, but relatively few taste their delights. The contrast of the lakeshore with the escarpment above ensures a comprehensive acquaintance with the Screes, and both these complementary legs offer more drama than anticipated. There is just one rough bouldery section on the lakeshore path, but this is entertaining and time-consuming rather than dangerous.

S Rejoin the access road alongside the car park, which leads to a bridge on Lingmell Gill, looking over the head of Wastwater. Bear right at the junction on the farm road which leads by the lakeshore to Wasdale Head Hall. As it turns up to the farm, take a stile in front and cross a couple of lakeside pastures to the base of Illgill Head. A good path heads away, and remains our route for the full length of the lake.

Throughout this the views are quite superb, most notably to Yewbarrow above the lonely farmstead of Bowderdale, with Haycock and Red Pike behind: remember also to look back to see Yewbarrow taking greater shape, while further back still is Great Gable's noble profile. Keeping mostly some way above the water's edge, the path is a delightful stroll far from the crowds. Several short stretches of scree are encountered, which the well stamped path makes light work of.

All has been progressing well until, on suddenly rounding a corner, a chaotic tumble of boulders awaits, a truly challenging prospect. The path can be forgotten for this quarter-mile: simply pick a way across the massive blocks. Those adept at boulder hopping will consider this a breeze, and certainly easier than the shifting scree paths encountered on some fellwalks. Others will teeter gingerly along, but there is consolation in the fact that most of these rocks are so immense they are unlikely to move anywhere! It is intriguing to consider that the fall of the Screes is so enthusiastic that on reaching the lakeshore they continue more than 200 feet further to the bed of the lake.

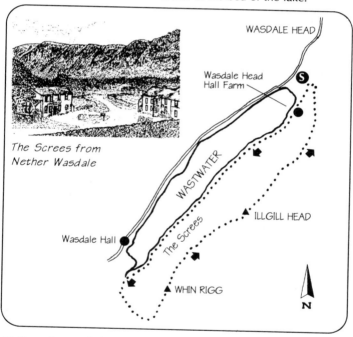

The Screes from
Nether Wasdale

At the other end the path reforms, and off we go as if it never happened. The last stage is a grand finish over tame scree, with Wasdale Hall (a youth hostel) in its grounds across the narrowing lakefoot. The end comes at a pumping station, so head off along its access road. Reaching a gate, don't pass through but retain the open fell by turning left up the wallside. A path traces the wall around to the foot of tree-lined Greathall Gill. Don't enter this deep ravine, but turn left to commence the half hour's steep work onto the open slopes. Immediately the views open out over the foot of the lake, to the village of Nether Wasdale, with woodland and fields leading out to the coast, and quite often the Isle of Man.

A well worn path winds up the slope, and on easing out at a large prominent cairn, continues up to become fainter and ultimately meet a clearer path at a T-junction by a cairn. Looking seawards again, the long line of Muncaster Fell above lower Eskdale is backed by the extensive multiple estuary at Ravenglass. Turn left on the new path for a steady rise to the top of Whin Rigg. Tops to left and right vie for supremacy, the slightly more distant right one having the finest cairn and probably the highest ground, the nearer left one having a shelter.

A whole new scene is revealed now, with Scafell ahead, Crinkle Crags to the right beyond Burnmoor Tarn, and the Coniston Fells and Harter Fell further round. Whin Rigg is the lesser known counterpart of Illgill Head, but forms one half of the renowned Wastwater Screes. Indeed, its cliffs and gullies are superior to those further along the ridge. Illgill Head waits surprisingly tamely to the north, for the rear of the Screes proves to be a modest place indeed.

Heading north, within two minutes the path rounds the head of Great Gully, the first of many encountered by remaining near the edge. This one affords a bird's-eye view of the lakefoot and Wasdale Hall. Not all steps trace the edge, and in poor weather it may be wiser to take the direct path through the saddle, passing a tarn before the short rise onto Illgill Head. However, the finest way to link these two tops will always be along the thinner path tracing the rim of the escarpment. Most of the finest moments come early in this walk, where promontories project invitingly out above the gullies and spiky ridges to add further drama to an already inspiring scene. But beware of complacency on these flat, grassy platforms above vertical rock walls!

However approached it is a steady rise onto Illgill Head, ultimately bearing right to a cairn which is assumed as the top. On gaining it, the true top is revealed a few minutes further, across a broad ridge now well away from the edge. A shelter occupies the top, though on looking back, the South top's cairn now appears decidedly higher! Like other fells that narrowly fail to reach a certain height, Illgill Head is probably more than happy to remain below 2000ft, thus escaping many pairs of boots.

Leave Illgill Head by continuing north on the main path, dropping gently to a cairned knoll before commencing one of the easiest descents in the district. Marked by odd cairns, the path ambles down this rounded grassy end in the direction of Great Gable. Throughout this we are treated to a superb picture of the Wasdale Head scene, indeed probably the best overview of its mountain setting. Dropping to meet an old wall, cross and resume down with it. Burnmoor Tarn appears over to the right, backed by shapely Harter Fell. The path curves down to the left to then cross the wall in front of Straighthead Gill.

After crossing the beck the path merges into the old corpse road coming over Burnmoor from Eskdale, to descend together above Fence Wood. The pleasant track drops down past several ruins (please ensure the bridle-gates are firmly closed behind you) onto easier grassy terrain, passing beneath the climbing hut at Brackenclose. Just beyond it the Scafells path is met alongside Lingmell Gill, and the bridge where we began is just below.

Wastwater and the Screes

> ### SUMMITS
> YEWBARROW   2057ft/627m
> STIRRUP CRAG   2021ft/616m

START Wastwater   **Grid ref.** NY 168068

DISTANCE 4 miles/6½ km   **ASCENT** 1952ft/595m

ORDNANCE SURVEY MAPS
1:50,000 - Landranger 89   1:25,000 - Outdoor Leisure 6

ACCESS Start from the National Trust car park at Overbeck Bridge, by the lakeshore less than 2 miles south of Wasdale Head.

No-one travelling the lakeside road to Wasdale Head can mistake Yewbarrow, narrowing to a perfect cone and for long enough appearing to overtop the equally shapely Great Gable, when in reality the more distant mountain is almost half as tall again. This, however, does not detract from a memorable little fellwalk. Note that some downward scrambling is required at the far end of the ridge beneath Stirrup Crag, though one could quite happily retrace the ascent route.

S From the car park a path runs by Over Beck to a gate to begin what looks an unremitting climb up the ridge of Yewbarrow. In the company of the fence/wall a pleasant green path proves far less demanding than anticipated, while the views back over Wastwater to the famous Screes are quite superb. A charming feature is the delightful view back down to Bowderdale's neatly packaged emerald fields in a surround of fell country. On reaching a stile the path escapes left to avoid confrontation with the craggy bluff of Bell Rib.

A branch continuing left is the return path, but the main path slants higher to be faced with Dropping Crag. Climbing soon restarts up a stony shoot that narrows to squeeze between crags, more scrambling opportunities arising before an easier pull to a memorable arrival at the Great Door. This famous gash in the mountain frames a splendid full-length prospect of the Scafells looming across this brief knife-edge section of the ridge. Before the climb to the Great Door, a well trodden path breaks off left to omit this classic moment, gaining the ridge at a similar, less inspiring notch. Several minor outcrops interrupt what becomes a grassy and increasingly gentle stroll up to the summit cairn, located a long way back from the action. In the grassy sea of an extensive, undulating plateau, compensation comes in the form of Great Gable and the Scafells looking as majestic as ever.

STIRRUP CRAG

WASDALE HEAD

YEWBARROW

Bowderdale

Overbeck Bridge **S**

WASTWATER

N

The path continues north along the broad ridge, crossing a depression before a short pull to the cairn on Stirrup Crag. Relax and savour the view from here, for lurking not far beneath the cairn is one of the more interesting obstacles on Lakeland ridges. The continuing path quickly leads to the start of a fascinating descent, first twisting down to another cairn as eyes are fixed on the grassy saddle of Dore Head, several hundred feet below. Apprehension mounts as the top of the crag is reached, from where eyes are better fixed on the task in hand.

This rock barrier initially appears impassable when hovering on the brink above, and it comes as a surprise to find that excepting icy conditions, this scrambly descent is not fraught with difficulties. A well worn route spirals down a clever series of chimneys and clefts between bands of rock, hands not being the only parts of the anatomy to be pressed into service. All too soon the escapade is over, and the path zigzags down through scree to deposit you abruptly onto the grassy saddle of Dore Head. Much satisfaction will be gained in pausing to look back from the sanctuary of this broad col.

Ahead, the climb to Red Pike can be incorporated by transferring to WALK 11. However, the gentle half of the descent begins by dropping left on a rapidly improving path slanting down Yewbarrow's lower western flank. This runs for virtually a mile and a half at no more than a steady angle, parallel with Over Beck down to the right. Towards the bottom it passes beneath Dropping Crag to rejoin the outward path.

```
                    SUMMITS
          PILLAR   2926ft/892m
     LOOKING STEAD   2057ft/627m
```

START Wasdale Head   **Grid ref.** NY 187088

DISTANCE 7½ miles/12km   **ASCENT** 2755ft/840m

ORDNANCE SURVEY MAPS
1:50,000 - Landranger 89 **or** 90   1:25,000 - Outdoor Leisure 4 & 6

ACCESS Start from the spacious triangular green just before the road runs its final yards to the centre of the hamlet.

An extended climb to one of Lakeland's favourite mountains, made into something of a classic by virtue of the High Level Route, a remarkable traverse across the coves to the celebrated Pillar Rock. There is an easy alternative route to the relatively complex section.

S From the green advance along the narrow lane into the hamlet, and leave by the far side of the *Wasdale Head Inn*. Turn upstream past the superb example of a packhorse bridge, with Pillar already topping the Mosedale Horseshoe of fells beyond. At the end a gate admits to the open fell, and the main path bears off left with the wall. Here begins an easy amble into Mosedale, gaining little height as the side valley is entered. The green path then slants up through bracken to approach the environs of Gatherstone Beck. After a steeper climb the beck is crossed, followed by a series of zigzags (and the welcome addition of stone pitching) with the summit of Black Sail Pass up ahead. A long winding climb ensues up onto the crest of the pass. The top is marked by a long redundant and rather incongruous iron gate just beyond a large cairn.

Turn left with the fenceposts on a very steadily rising path. This largely avoids the dramatic northern edge, indeed it contours across the flank of the minor top Looking Stead, which might be incorporated during the return. At a well defined saddle overlooking the edge, the fenceposts are met after they drop back down from Looking Stead. Here a steeper climb begins, breaking its pull on a small knoll where a prominent cairn indicates the start of the High Level Route going off to the right. Those wanting the far easier and safer option can remain on the ridge, and set about the immediately steeper section in front.

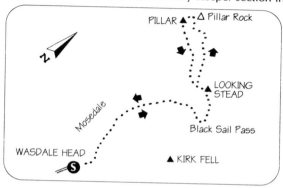

The High Level Route's name might well be called into question as it commences by dropping down, but it refers to its access to Pillar Rock, not the summit of the mountain. Certainly it seems to offer an improbable course across this craggy face, but after just a few downhill yards it settles down to a generally undulating course. A variety of terrain is encountered, from grassy terraces that appear little changed over half a century, to sensational moments above steep drops into Ennerdale. The going becomes gentler on entering the bouldery Hind Cove, at the end of which the guiding beacon of Robinson's Cairn stands proud.

The touching of this famous edifice is a stirring moment as Pillar Rock appears in all its glory across Pillar Cove. Pillar Rock is the feature that named the mountain, and is one of the grandest objects in the district as it projects itself from the fell high above Ennerdale. As the path sets off it dips across the cove, with some fine pinnacles towering above. After a short climb through scree turn right along the Shamrock Traverse, a broad, tilted ledge that precedes a clamber up the side of a sloping slab. Atop this the path arrives at a splendid viewing station, and now on equal terms, the rockface can be visually explored in fascinating detail.

A little terrace leads round to the very neck where the Rock is attached to the mountain. From here the path turns to enjoy a thoroughly enjoyable climb to the summit, these last several hundred feet being a first-class finale to what the High Level Route began. When faced with a short scramble up a direct gully, an easier option goes right and curves up to the plateau edge at a shelter, but the scramble makes a more appropriate conclusion. The going suddenly relents and the path eases itself onto Pillar's surprisingly extensive summit plateau. A multi-angled shelter in the centre marks the highest point some 60 yards away, alongside an Ordnance Survey column and a cairn. Such a broad summit repays an exploration of its rim, where fine aspects await of Ennerdale Water, Scoat Fell and Steeple, and of course the emphatic plunge of the Ennerdale face.

Depart the summit to the south-east, a path forming within yards, aided by fenceposts. In good weather be sure to savour the awesome views over the northern edges, not all of which are seen if holding to the path. The clear path keeps generally close to the line of defunct fenceposts during this extended amble down the prolonged east ridge to Black Sail Pass. With a good mile of the ridge underfoot, the Looking Stead col is regained, and the fenceposts can be followed up onto the grassy summit dome. The cairned top awaits just one minute from the main path, and makes a perfect viewing platform for Pillar Rock's setting. The old posts will lead back to the path just short of the pass, and outward steps can be retraced to Wasdale Head.

Pillar from Row Head packhorse bridge, Wasdale Head

> **SUMMITS**
> KIRK FELL   2631ft/802m
> KIRK FELL EAST TOP   2582ft/787m

START Wasdale Head   **Grid ref.** NY 187088

DISTANCE 5½ miles/9km   **ASCENT** 2690ft/820m

ORDNANCE SURVEY MAPS
1:50,000 - Landranger 89 **or** 90   1:25,000 - Outdoor Leisure 4 & 6

ACCESS Start from the spacious triangular green just before the road runs its final yards to the centre of the hamlet.

An unswervingly steep climb featuring rough scree towards the top makes this a less than elegant ascent, but on a clear day the permanently first-class views will enthral. This is also one of the less frequented Wasdale fells.

S From the green advance along the narrow lane into the hamlet, and leave by the far side of the *Wasdale Head Inn*. Turn upstream past a fine example of a packhorse bridge, with the Mosedale Horseshoe of fells beyond. Ahead, however, our own Kirk Fell takes on an uncompromising stance. At the end a gate admits to the open fell, and the ascent, begins here, instantly! As the Black Sail path bears off left with the wall, simply continue straight up in front, a path leading unfailingly up Kirk Fell's unrelenting contours. Little description is needed, though there will be ample halts to savour the view, with the Wasdale Head scene being outstanding from the outset.

Ultimately a grassy knoll brings everyone to a welcome halt, then the upper section leads into scree, much of which is inescapable. The path scrabbles steeply and ungainly up the rivers of stones, and an escape onto grass comes with much relief. A higher level scree section is far less intimidating, and this leads to a small but inviting arete. Atop this the going eases and the terrors are over, a grassy slope being virtually pathless as cairns guide the way onto the extensive, intermittently grassy and stony top. Simply continue straight up to find the summit. A circular shelter occupies the highest point, with a cairn on lower ground 25 yards to its north.

Though Kirk Fell is uniformly steep on all sides, instead of tapering to a peak to rival Great Gable, the slopes disappointingly falter at a crucial stage, resulting in a top so extensive it manages two different summits. In spite of its girth this is a superb viewpoint, with Wastwater and its Screes and the Scafell grouping well seen. Pride of place goes to Gable, whose proximity exaggerates its grotesquely contorted form from this unique angle, as if the top few hundred feet have been twisted like the top of a paper bag.

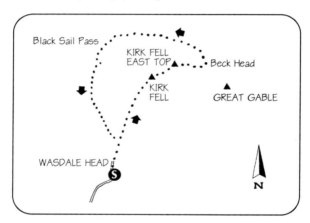

While there may be great satisfaction in gaining Kirk Fell's summit, there will be less after considering only a mile and a half has been covered! So to make a fuller walk of it, a circuitous but rewarding higher level section ensues. Only yards north of the cairn the fenceposts of the Ennerdale watershed are met, and these can be comfortably followed north-east in poor visibility. They run north of Kirkfell Tarn and up to gain the summit of Kirk Fell's cairned East Top. Alternatively, drop down to pass between the tarn and its southerly pool, then make the five minute climb of the slopes behind to gain the East Top. Note that a path of sorts outflanks this top to its south.

Depart eastwards with the fenceposts, and a faint path strides across easy ground to a well defined edge. Here a broad, stony path clambers down Bell Rib, easing out to deposit you onto Beck Head. Mighty Gable looms directly in front, but at this point turn your back on it. In the grassy saddle turn down left to a cairn on a boulder between Beck Head's two reedy pools, and yards beneath it a clear path forms to double back under Kirk Fell's flank.

Its aim is to traverse the northern flank of the mountain to Black Sail Pass, while losing as little height as possible. This it does most successfully, being a super path in a grand mountain setting. With towering cliffs above and Ennerdale far below, the path ambles delightfully on. A little height is lost as the pass summit and path climbing to it from Ennerdale are seen ahead, and our path swings in to cross the impressive ravine of Sail Beck. The path then climbs more directly for the few minutes needed to gain the crest of Black Sail Pass. This is marked by a long redundant and rather incongruous iron gate, and, to the Wasdale side, a large cairn.

From this junction of paths turn left, a few yards on to the cairn to commence the return to Wasdale. The path quickly sets about its task,

descending roughly with Mosedale far below. With the welcome addition of stone pitching during 1998, a series of zigzags work down to cross Gatherstone Beck, and easier going slants down to the base of the fell. The path meanders on at length along the edge of Mosedale to return to the point were the fell was gained, just five minutes from the end.

Napes Needle window,
St. Olaf's church,
Wasdale Head

```
            SUMMITS
GREAT GABLE   2949ft/899m
```

START Wasdale Head   **Grid ref.** NY 187088

DISTANCE 6½ miles/10½km   **ASCENT** 2625ft/800m

ORDNANCE SURVEY MAPS
1:50,000 - Landranger 89 **or** 90   1:25,000 - Outdoor Leisure 6

ACCESS Start from the spacious triangular green just before the road runs its final yards to the centre of the hamlet.

A pilgrimage to a famous summit. As this walk is almost exclusively on the Wasdale flank of the mountain, there are largely unbroken views down the valley and across Wastwater from a rare variety of foregrounds. The route described features some rough walking and a scree climb, though there is no obligatory scrambling of any note (from Sty Head one can in any case opt for a direct, uncomplicated route to the top).

S   The walk leaves the green by the rough lane past the church, which can also be reached by fieldpath directly from the hamlet. The walled lane runs to Burnthwaite, and already enjoys superb views of this mountain surround, with Pillar and the Mosedale Horseshoe to the left, Kirk Fell and Great Gable in front, Great End and Lingmell to the right, and back to Illgill Head and Wastwater. At the farm pass left of the buildings and a broad track bears right, running through emerald pastureland between widely spaced walls.

Emerging adjacent to the wide stony bed of Lingmell Beck, the way runs on to a footbridge over inflowing Gable Beck. Across it a cairn sees Moses' Trod begin its climb to Beck Head, but as that is for the return, keep straight on. Great Gable looms ahead as only Gable can, and the ascent path across its lower south face is equally unmissable. Ignoring any lesser branches, simply remain on this broad path as it sets about the slopes, soon passing through a gate in a wall. All the while the views across the side valley of Lingmell Beck are quite superb, with Piers Gill taking shape on Lingmell's flank, and a constantly improving backdrop of the mighty Scafell group.

A particularly stony section is encountered where a series of streams tumble across the path. Look up to the left here to see the Cat or Sphinx Rock nicely silhouetted; up above, the South Traverse - though its line is not visible - awaits. Just beyond, the path eases out on a grassy plinth, with the cliff of Kern Knotts directly above. A little further and a corner is rounded to a big cairn. Just past this the boulder and attendant stretcher box on Sty Head are reached with ease, as the path leads onto the crest of one of the best known foot passes in the district.

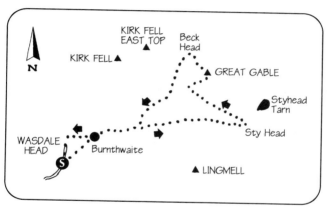

This is a meeting place of many routes, the most popular being the Breast Route making a direct ascent of Gable. If the rigours of the South Traverse and Little Hell Gate do not appeal, then simply set forth on this superbly restored route which will lead directly to the summit: when the restored section ends, the well cairned path remains easy to follow. Don't worry, there's no shame in it!

Just ten yards after the restored Breast Route sets off, a branch goes left, doubling back above our route thus far. There is a brief glimpse of Styhead Tarn from this grassy rise, then continuing, Kern Knotts appears just ahead, overtopped by the Great Napes. A cairn on a grassy alp just in front is a good place to survey the prospect before the path set off towards the rockface. Note the celebrated Kern Knotts Crack as the route traverses through boulders at the base of the crag. Beyond, cairns guide the way across more boulders, slanting up beneath some lower crags. Crossing a scree gully a nice easy stretch leads towards Tophet Bastion rearing ahead. Slant up to confront Great Hell Gate, the first of two mighty scree shoots that confine the massive crags of the Great Napes. Cross with ease to the very base of the crags.

Looking up Great Hell Gate, an impressively rough scene features the rock island of Hell Gate Pillar leading the eye towards Westmorland Crags. Immediately on rounding a corner, the Great Napes are more fully revealed, with the famous Napes Needle quite clear at the bottom left of the main crag. Another well known landmark is the Cat or Sphinx Rock, which appears up above, further along. At any forks the main path maintains the direct route, a largely level course which quickly arrives at a scree shoot coming out of Needle Gully: looking up, Napes Needle is now identified by the misleading overhang at its top.

If wishing to experience the Needle at close quarters turn up the scree gully, passing to the right of a chockstone and then, directly under the Needle, scramble left up onto the Dress Circle. As the safest continuation is to return the same way, be sure you are happy to repeat the scramble onto the Dress Circle in reverse. As its name implies, the Dress Circle is the perfect viewing platform for any climbing activity on the Needle, which is now seen in its traditional pose, backed by the Scafells.

Back down in the gully, continue along the South Traverse path, a grand little section passing through rock gates to drop down into Little Hell Gate, second of the mighty scree shoots. This is to be our passage to the summit. Note that if the rough scrabble up here does not appeal, one can simply cross the scree shoot and retain the South Traverse, which runs on again to Gavel Neese, and the path then contours round to Beck Head.

The route to the summit sets about Little Hell Gate. The best plan is to turn immediately uphill, keeping to its right side: here at least there are opportunities for respite by making use of some adjacent, solid rock. When level with a massive rock island, make a complete escape up a dank little gully. From here one can remain on grass all the way, easing out to suddenly emerge onto a grassy knoll above the crest of the Great Napes. Westmorland Crags, which seemed so distantly high up when in the gully, are now just a stone's throw above. Rise onto the crest to enjoy views to the east now, including the Langdale Pikes and Sprinkling Tarn. With the Hell Gates down either side turn along the grassy arete to the foot of Westmorland Crags, which the path swings left to outflank. At the top bear right to find the Westmorland Cairn, recalling two brothers of that name. This precariously balanced edifice is a famous landmark, its virtues as a viewpoint self-evident.

Great Gable (with Green Gable) from Innominate Tarn, Haystacks (on WALK 2)

The summit now awaits, just two minutes up the gentle slopes behind. This boulder-strewn felltop is without doubt one of Lakeland's favourite summits. As might be expected the complete panorama is absolutely superb, but the Scafell massif will always demand most attention. Great Gable shares with Scafell Pike an attraction for people who would normally never dream of venturing up a high mountain: this speaks volumes for the high regard in which it is held, for no-one can deny its magnetism. No other mountain in Lakeland so draws the eye, nor exerts such a mystical influence on the walker in the valley below. The highest feet of this characterful place are occupied by a final upthrust of rock, and a plaque records the gift of this and surrounding fells to the nation in memory of members of the Fell & Rock Climbing Club who gave their lives in the Great War: a remembrance service is conducted here each November.

Leave the top by heading north-west, aiming towards Haystacks and Crummock Water. Cairns guide the way, and as the ground steepens a clear path forms, with the grassy saddle of Beck Head appearing below. This descends roughly but pleasantly, though the path soon abdicates in favour of a line of cairns. The imposing cliff of Gable Crag appears back to the right. Easing out lower down, a clearer path returns, and the historic route of Moses' Trod comes in from the right. It is now just a short slant left down onto the saddle. Legend has it that Moses, a local quarryman, made use of this trade route through the hills, from Honister Pass to Wasdale Head, to smuggle his illicit whisky: we shall follow his steps back to the valley.

Although the path briefly fades, keep to the near side of the saddle - bound to the left for Wastwater - and a path quickly returns. Slanting down through stony surrounds, ignore a rougher drop to the right and remain on the gentler, intermittently slanting and level one. A path comes down from the South Traverse by way of the prominent Moses' Finger, an 8ft high pillar of rock: just below this junction, feet will take great relief in an abrupt transfer from stones to the grass of Gavel Neese.

A contrastingly grassy descent follows, with time to savour the Wasdale scene at one's feet. Remember to look back up to appraise Gable's rugged front, with the White Napes, Little Hell Gate, Westmorland Crags and Great Napes all featuring. Our grassy spur is also a splendid vantage point for the foliage-bedecked ravine of Ill Gill on Kirk Fell. The path runs down to a gate in a wall, from where the outward path is rejoined two minutes below.

The short mile to the hamlet can be varied at Burnthwaite. Instead of going through the gate at the farm, turn right along a green track enclosed by walls. This runs in delightful fashion, largely in the company of a stream, all the way back to join the Black Sail path at the foot of Kirk Fell. Turn left for two minutes along a footpath by Mosedale Beck, ending stylishly alongside the packhorse bridge behind the *Wasdale Head Inn*.

```
           SUMMITS
LINGMELL    2648ft/807m
```

START Wasdale Head   **Grid ref.** NY 187088

DISTANCE 5½ miles/9km   **ASCENT** 2415ft/736m

ORDNANCE SURVEY MAPS
1:50,000 - Landranger 89 **or** 90   1:25,000 - Outdoor Leisure 6

ACCESS Start from the spacious triangular green just before the road runs its final yards to the centre of the hamlet.

Lingmell's uniformly steep wall casts a dawn shadow over Wasdale Head, and to appreciate its finest aspect, this walk approaches it from the north. Here shattered cliffs plunge emphatically to the bold incision of Piers Gill, Lakeland's best known ravine. A return stroll down the west shoulder completes a grand outing amid spectacular mountain scenery.

S   The walk leaves the green by the rough lane past the church, which can also be reached by fieldpath directly from the *Wasdale Head Inn*. The walled lane runs to Burnthwaite, and already enjoys superb views of this mountain surround, with Pillar and the Mosedale Horseshoe to the left, Kirk Fell and Great Gable in front, Great End and Lingmell to the right, and back to Illgill Head and Wastwater. At the farm pass left of the buildings and a broad track bears right, running through emerald pastureland between widely spaced walls.

Emerging adjacent to the wide stony bed of Lingmell Beck, the way runs on to a footbridge over inflowing Gable Beck. Across it a cairn sees Moses' Trod begin its climb to Beck Head, but keep straight on. 200 yards further, a less obvious fork is reached. While the main arm rises across Great Gable's flank, opt for the fainter way keeping faith with the beck.

This latter option is an easy stroll into the heart of the mountains, with Great End now more dominant straight ahead and the Great Napes on Gable towering above. A few cairns guide the way across a series of side-streams to approach the major confluence of Spouthead Gill from the left and Piers Gill under the watchful eye of Lingmell. Around this point Scafell Pike's lofty neighbour Broad Crag briefly reveals itself, tantalisingly high beyond the turrets above Piers Gill.

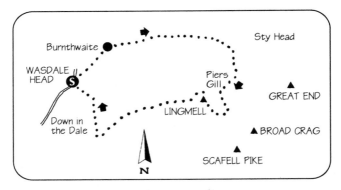

The path crosses Spouthead Gill 100 yards above the confluence, and zigzags up the grassy tongue in between. As Piers Gill swings off to the right, the main path is again forsaken in favour of a right branch, an initially very faint way which keeps well above the beck. This soon becomes clearer if still intermittent to rise to cross the next side-stream of Greta Gill just above its confluence. On the right now the ravine of Piers Gill takes shape, and the path keeps well above the edge of this magnificent cleft: minor diversions are needed to peer into the ravine, but not to appraise the jagged pinnacles topping Lingmell Crag. Lingmell and Piers Gill are illustrated on page 72.

Approaching the distinct dog-leg of Piers Gill, a delightful scramble with ample holds climbs more directly above the gill. With the ravine for company again the path climbs more gently to meet the Corridor Route from Sty Head just as it crosses the upper ravine. Take great care here as accidents are not unknown around this point. Turning right, it first crosses the head of the ravine, and then rather oddly the stream itself. The upper 500 feet of Scafell Pike rise splendidly in front, with Broad Crag to its left. The main path bound more directly for the Pike is soon left on a slimmer, cairned trod across a green hollow on the right, rising with and crossing a ruinous wall to gain the Lingmell Col. A short pull up the path to the right will quickly have Lingmell's summit underfoot, the highest point being crowned by a splendidly constructed cairn.

Lingmell's view is inevitably constrained by its neighbours, though this works to advantage as it could well have been specially sited as a viewing platform for the Wasdale giants. Despite its proximity, the Scafell massif is ranged magnificently, while the prospect of Great Gable speaks for itself. If respite be needed from the mountains, there is always Wastwater leading the eye to the coast, and the contrasting attractions of Windscale (sorry, Sellafield) and the Isle of Man.

The return route is made down the broad west ridge. The quickest start departs the cairn by heading a little south of west down initially stony, part-cairned slopes, aiming for the minor knoll just ahead. In clear weather, a brief detour is first recommended: with Great Gable not being quite as well displayed as might be expected, drop briefly north-west to a craftsman-built pillar in view from the summit. This earns the classic full-frontal picture of mighty Gable. Now swing back to contour beneath the summit area and aim for Wastwater. Throughout much of this descent, however, it is the prospect of Scafell that holds the attention. A clearer path forms on grassy terrain to surmount the minor intervening knoll.

On the knoll the old wall is re-crossed before a steady, cairned descent through further stones. Below this it's a leisurely amble down the broad grassy ridge, made all the more special in view of the general roughness of the surrounding fells. Illgill Head tumbles into Wastwater directly ahead; the Mosedale Horseshoe features to the right; while a summer's evening projects an enchanting light on the Scafells' crags. At the nose end the entire lake is now in view, and with all of Wasdale Head on show, this is surely the finest viewpoint for this famous setting. A steeper, stony drop now ensues, but grassy ways soon return to arrive at a wall crossing the ridge.

Across the ladder-stile enjoy the lazy grassy path continuing down through the bracken of the lower ridge to join the path out of Lingmell Gill. Turn right on this for an easy angled slant down to a footbridge on Lingmell Beck. This final section is a riot of colour when hawthorn and gorse display their springtime flowers. Cross straight over the pasture to a stile onto the road, just a minute short of the green.

```
         SUMMITS
GREAT END    2986ft/910m
ILL CRAG    3068ft/935m
BROAD CRAG    3064ft/934m
SCAFELL PIKE    3209ft/978m
```

START Wasdale Head   **Grid ref.** NY 187088

DISTANCE 8 miles/13km   **ASCENT** 3500ft/1067m

ORDNANCE SURVEY MAPS
1:50,000 - Landranger 89 or 90   1:25,000 - Outdoor Leisure 6

ACCESS Start from the spacious triangular green just before the road runs its final yards to the centre of the hamlet.

England's loftiest peak is also perhaps its finest: only Great Gable could make similar claims to the crown. As such it deserves a fitting ascent, and this finest of routes makes a high level approach from Sty Head by way of the Band, Great End, Ill Crag and Broad Crag.

S   The walk leaves the green by the rough lane past the church, which can also be reached by fieldpath directly from the hamlet. The walled lane runs to Burnthwaite, and already enjoys superb views of this mountain surround, with Pillar and the Mosedale Horseshoe to the left, Kirk Fell and Great Gable in front, Great End and Lingmell to the right, and back to Illgill Head and Wastwater. At the farm pass left of the buildings and a broad track bears right, running through emerald pastureland between widely spaced walls.

Emerging adjacent to the wide stony bed of Lingmell Beck, the way runs on to a footbridge over inflowing Gable Beck. Across it a cairn sees Moses' Trod begin its climb to Beck Head, but keep straight on. 200 yards further, a less obvious fork is reached. While the main arm rises across Great Gable's flank, opt for the fainter way keeping faith with the beck. This latter option is an easy stroll into the heart of the mountains, with Great End now more dominant straight ahead and the Great Napes on Gable towering above. A few cairns guide the way across a series of side-streams to approach the major confluence of Spouthead Gill from the left and Piers Gill under the watchful eye of Lingmell. Around this point Scafell Pike's lofty neighbour Broad Crag briefly reveals itself, tantalisingly high beyond the turrets above Piers Gill.

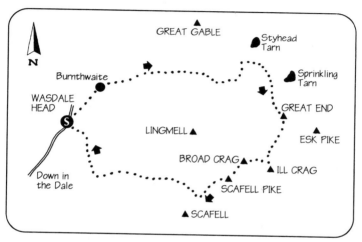

The path crosses Spouthead Gill 100 yards above the confluence, and zigzags up the grassy tongue in between. As Piers Gill swings off to the right, the main path continues its superb grassy zigzags, re-crossing the southern arm of Spouthead Gill and then on up to cross its northern arm into a green bowl. A line of cairns in the lush green turf send a path right, but this rises to the Corridor Route beneath the great gash of Skew Gill: instead bear left on another path which has a curiously brief built section before rising to quickly emerge onto Sty Head. The summit of the pass is marked by a massive boulder and a stretcher box at a junction of popular paths. Styhead Tarn appears just as the crest is gained, backed by the first new sighting to the north, a distant Blencathra.

While Great Gable rises to the left of the pass, the steep slopes of Great End hover to the right: this hoary mountain is an integral member of the Scafell group, forming an abrupt northern buttress to the highest ridgeline in England. Only a direct ascent up the Band can do it true justice. At Sty Head a right turn (eastwards) takes the broad path bound for Esk Hause. Directly ahead is the bony rib of the Band tumbling from the summit plateau of Great End, and this spur provides a natural and rewarding stairway to the top. Whilst a very faint path breaks off the Esk Hause path just before crossing the parallel beck, the purist's route involves tackling the Band immediately, and outflanking several small outcrops before a tiny saddle signals the arrival of the aforementioned path. On this ascent, each pause for rest finds new features appearing in the expanding view. On this occasion, notable landmarks include Sprinkling Tarn, the Glaramara ridge, Skiddaw, Dale Head, Derwentwater and Grisedale Pike.

The path takes a fairly clear line up the Band, pausing for respite at a little trough marking the start of the great ravine of Skew Gill, though not apparent as such. Here Pillar appears to the west, overtopping Kirk Fell. Above this point the going roughens a little, hardly surprising in view of the intimidating slopes above - though there is no cause for panic. A very early little scramble faces us, though the main path finds

Lingmell and Piers Gill from near Sty Head

an easier way to the right. Simply pick a way up through the boulders, with many easy and very enjoyable optional scrambles being found to the right of the path. As the path itself becomes steeper and stonier, the more rewarding bouldery option to its right becomes increasingly irresistible.

The drama culminates on a slabby platform, where the well worn path climbs from the left, on the near side of a gully with exceedingly craggy slopes behind. A gentler rise now leads onto the north-west cairn, which with its adjacent shelter makes a splendid viewpoint for Wasdale and Great Gable. Also greeting the eye is the uppermost ground of England, the high, bouldery ridge of Scafell Pike and its trusty satellites Ill Crag and Broad Crag. Despite being little over 200 feet superior, England's premier mountain still succeeds in appearing absolutely monstrous.

Across a minor depression on this broad, stony top waits the marginally higher summit cairn. En route, keep left to inspect the dramatic upper reaches of a sombre network of cliffs and gullies, from which an aerial view of Sprinkling Tarn leads the eye into Borrowdale; the finest feature is the rift of Central Gully, a popular winter ascent route (for the experienced and equipped) which gains the plateau just yards short of the summit. New aspects of the view eastwards include the Langdale Pikes and the long Helvellyn skyline.

In the saddle on Great End's plateau a cairned path forms to drop gently down to meet the more populated Esk Hause-Scafell Pike path at the Calf Cove col. After a stony climb onto the shoulder of Ill Crag, easier going may tempt a detour left to Ill Crag's beckoning summit. This will guarantee a little further solitude, but more importantly earn stunning views into the unfrequented haven of Upper Eskdale, with a lower top perched even more dramatically above the valley head. This is also a useful vantage point for appraising the position of Broad Crag in relation to the massif.

From Ill Crag curve back round to rejoin the main path in the Ill Crag col, and after a slight rise across Broad Crag's shoulder, devotees of rough ground will revel in the briefest of detours onto what is positively the roughest mountain summit in Lakeland. A neat cairn occupies the highest of the massive boulders on this remarkable blocky top. With caution it is an even shorter drop back onto the path, with the final saddle, the Broad Crag col, just below. The final climb starts rough and stony, and ends by crossing the bouldery uppermost slopes of England's highest acres to gain the highest point, a mighty platform that rises above all else.

The roughnesses of Scafell Pike are legend, the summit minefield of boulders being a natural obstacle course. The country's highest ground is celebrated by a solid stone platform, with steps built in to enable zealous visitors to steal a few artificial feet. Accepting defeat, an Ordnance Survey column cowers a few steps away. The unparalleled glut of building materials has been put to further use to construct a range of shelters, those to the east of the summit resembling miniature sheepfolds.

To add to its list of credits, the Pike stands at the epicentre of the best of mountain Lakeland, surrounded by such loyal subjects as Bowfell, Scafell and Gable, and with the untamed wilderness of the upper Esk on one side and the deep void of Wasdale on the other. Here is a mountain that lives up to its reputation. There are no forgettable days on the Pike.

So often in shadow when viewed from Scafell Pike is the craggy face of neighbouring Scafell, to the south, and our first objective, also in view, is the narrow, connecting ridge of Mickledore. Leave the summit by taking the main cairned way, west, but within 200 yards take the slightly less obvious left fork at a profusely cairned junction. Note that in poor visibility it is better to stay on the 'tourist' path down towards the Lingmell Col, then swinging left just before it to drop down to meet our route above Brown Tongue.

For Mickledore, however, the left branch descends steadily to this unique saddle, a short-lived ridge that whilst linking with Scafell, also denies direct access to it. Cause of this impasse is Scafell Crag, the masterpiece of rock architecture now seen to such good advantage. Famous features such as Broad Stand and Lord's Rake can be easily identified, but it is the sheer might of the crag itself that will be remembered. The presence of a stretcher box should be sufficient warning that in this vicinity there are more situations than usual in which to come unstuck.

In the very nick a massive cairn sends a very rough path down to the right. At once the wall of Pulpit Rock on Pikes Crag enters the scene on the right. As the trying path quickly opens out, opt to zigzag as best one can, and the hard work is soon over on being deposited into the grassy amphitheatre of Hollow Stones. A lengthy pause is merited here to savour the atmosphere of our rock walled prison, with both Scafell Crag and Pikes Crag hovering menacingly above: awesome stuff.

As the path resumes, much of the remaining descent is on restored sections, initially through eroded scree of the old path. The direct descent path merges in from the right, and there is much pleasure in these relaxing, grassy surrounds having witnessed so much rough and rocky terrain; ahead, Wastwater itself increasingly attracts attention. Merging with a sidestream, the superbly built path shadows it down beneath the spur of Brown Tongue to a confluence with Lingmell Gill. Looking back up the tongue, the line of its abandoned, scarred path can be seen to be recovering well.

At the confluence Lingmell Gill is crossed in a charming setting, before descending with the lively stream to a kissing-gate. Through it, take a contouring path branching right. This gains the base of Lingmell's west ridge and provides a superb moment as the Wasdale Head scene returns ahead, the cosy hamlet being backed as ever by Pillar. The path commences an easy angled slant down to a footbridge on Lingmell Beck. This final section is a riot of colour when the hawthorn and gorse display their springtime flowers. Cross straight over the pasture to a stile onto the road, just a minute short of the green.

Lingmell, Scafell Pike and Scafell from Wastwater

21

SCAFELL

```
┌─────────────────────────────────────┐
│              SUMMITS                 │
│  SYMOND'S KNOTT   3146ft/959m        │
│     SCAFELL   3163ft/964m            │
│   SLIGHT SIDE   2499ft/762m          │
└─────────────────────────────────────┘
```

START Eskdale   **Grid ref.** NY 200009

DISTANCE 10½ miles/17km   **ASCENT** 3035ft/925m

ORDNANCE SURVEY MAPS
1:50,000 - Landranger 89 **or** 90   1:25,000 - Outdoor Leisure 6

ACCESS Start from the valley road above Wha House Farm, a long mile and a half east of Boot, just past the youth hostel. There is a parking area immediately above the road. Dalegarth station at Boot is the terminus of the Ravenglass & Eskdale Railway from Ravenglass, on the Cumbrian Coast railway.

The rewards for climbing the country's second highest mountain from Eskdale are, quite simply, incalculable. From a first-class, crowd-free approach through a tangle of colourful slopes, to Lakeland's greatest wilderness in the upland amphitheatre of Great Moss, featuring an intimate look at the little seen Cam Spout Crag and adjacent falls, and the unparalleled grandeur of what is the finest mountain scene in England.

S From the parking area head east along the road for a couple of minutes, then bear left along the drive to Taw House. Early steps are dominated by the splendid Harter Fell across the valley, and its pass straight ahead. At the farm a permissive path takes the first gate on the left on entering, to avoid the yards and fields. A path then runs along the top side of the wall on the base of the fell, with early prospects of Bowfell from either side of the farm. This splendid green path runs on to cross tree-lined Scale Beck on the stone arched Scale Bridge, which makes a good vantage point for the falls immediately upstream.

When the path forks 100 yards further, bear left, slanting grandly up beneath Heron Crag. This splendid old way zigzags stylishly up the fellside, and at the top the path resumes our orderly northward march. Within five minutes a corner is turned to reveal an awesome prospect as Esk Pike, Bowfell and Crinkle Crags are joined by the stunningly arrayed Slight Side, Scafell Pike and Ill Crag - a champagne moment.

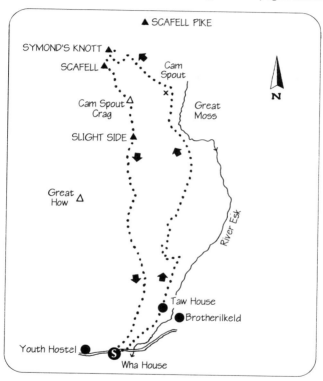

The path now runs a near level course for a considerable time, the full length of the left side of a long marsh. Simply keep straight on this smashing path until the gentlest of brows is crossed, and just past a small, lower marsh the sanctuary of Great Moss is revealed, surrounded by the finest peaks in the land. Also worth picking out are the cliffs of Cam Spout Crag on Scafell's slopes, and Esk Buttress (Dow

Crag on maps) on Scafell Pike's slopes. In between the two is Cam Spout, key to our ascent. The path drops left, curving round to pass through a sheepfold followed by the boulders of Sampson's Stones beneath Cam Spout Crag.

Just a few minutes further the path runs beneath bouldery slopes to arrive at Cam Spout. At this major staging post the rambling ends and the climbing begins. Linger well to admire the delightful falls, then set about the real stuff after crossing the stream. The first stage is an extended, very easy scramble, which the main path initially avoids on the right. The tilted slabs alongside the falls make light work of uphill progress, and on easing out Scafell finally reveals its true self, as does the great pass of Mickledore linking it with the magnificent Scafell Pike. The path rises through a confluence and up the tongue into the bowl, a wonderful place to be.

Approaching the base of the crags a less obvious cairned, grassier path breaks off left from the main path bound for Mickledore. At the foot of the crag it is joined by a scree path slanting down from Mickledore. Here turn left up a well defined gully, clambering up boulders which make for rapid and absorbing progress. This dead-straight line between rock walls offers some optional scrambling, and on emerging, it maintains the same line to arrive at the hollow of Foxes Tarn. The tarn itself is a tiny pool half-filled by a large boulder, but it is a grand place to be.

The final section is a surprisingly easy one, by virtue of the exceptionally well built path zigzagging up otherwise tortuous scree slopes all the way onto Scafell's summit plateau. While the cairn stands just up to the left, first bear right, in good conditions, to 'see the sights'. Just two minutes away is the head of Deep Gill, from where the sheer walls of Scafell's crags are displayed in no uncertain terms. Across the gully rises the majestic Scafell Pinnacle, while the spectacularly sited top of Symond's Knott hovers to the left on top of Deep Gill Buttress.

A rocky clamber leads to the cairn on Symond's Knott, a delectable perch from which to gaze down over the cragtops into the fearful abyss. While Wastwater and the Pillar group are suddenly revealed in style, it is the rock architecture beneath one's feet that will stay in the memory. Symond's Knott, incidentally, recalls the Rev. H. H. Symonds, early guidebook writer and a founder of the Friends of the Lake District.

Having devoured the grandeur return across the saddle where several paths unite for the two minute pull onto Scafell's summit cairn. From this stony top Symond's Knott appears of equal height and far more deserving of summit status. Across the undetectable void of Mickledore the solid-looking top of the Pike asserts its superiority to a far greater extent than the mere 50 or so feet that separate this celebrated pair. As a viewpoint Scafell is extensive rather than exciting. Burnmoor Tarn shimmers on one side, above Wastwater, while on the other side are the upper recesses of Eskdale.

Scafell Pinnacle with Great Gable beyond, from the top of Deep Gill

Leave by heading south along the stony ridge, which within a minute reveals Slight Side below, and equally quickly the minor top of Cam Spout Crag nearer, to its left. Keep to the highest ground, a largely clear path drops down to a grassy saddle and the faintest of rises leads to the cairn atop Cam Spout Crag. This really is an outstanding platform from which to survey the Scafells scene, including in the foreground our route from Cam Spout. Resuming, a briefly stony slope precedes a short, easy walk along to Slight Side. Probably the least visited of the Scafell group tops, this marks the sudden termination of Scafell's south ridge, and thus the end of this walk's drama.

The summit is Slight Side's *raison d'etre*, consisting of twin rock bosses split by a narrow defile. The highest is the cairned one on the right (west). The view also plays its part in the top's appeal, and stresses Slight Side's affinity with Eskdale. From here the entire valley is gazed upon, the course of this most beautiful river being traced from the near wilderness of its beginnings beneath the highest mountains, through the colourful mid-valley country below Harter Fell and Hard Knott, and finally to its brief lazy miles preceding entry into the Irish Sea at the all-embracing estuary at Ravenglass.

The path passes through the gap and slants left to avoid craggy ground. Ignore an early, eroded branch right, and continue down the slimmer way which swings back right to slant down, a little stonily, onto grassy slopes. This marks the end of any roughnesses, and a thin but clear path resumes down the gentle grassy slopes, intermittently cairned and angling slightly left as it goes. This proves to be a super stroll, with Harter Fell straight in front, returning to take some shape and claim greater importance as height is slowly lost. Approaching the marshy Cowcove basin the path turns along to the right, traversing high above it and running along to the smaller, higher level Catcove basin. Though occasionally faint the presence of cairns dispels any doubts as to the path's course.

Pass along the right side of the marsh, and as the stream drops through a ravine at the end, keep straight on. This remains the course for some time, on and on without ever encountering steep ground. Another marshy basin is wisely crossed at the outset, and at the end there is a glimpse of Brotherilkeld farm down to the left. Cross the outflowing trickle to resume as before; not for nothing is the splendid path known as the Terrace Route.

The path angles down to reveal the environs of Brotherilkeld more fully now, the green fields of the valley floor contrasting with our colourful immediate surrounds. Only grudgingly does the path join the wall below, ultimately dropping to a wall corner-cum-sheepfold. The finish is now just five minutes away, and is quickly revealed below as we slant down to a stile in the fence at the parking area, a bull's-eye finish!

HARD KNOTT

```
┌─────────────────────────────────┐
│          SUMMITS                │
│   HARD KNOTT   1801ft/549m      │
└─────────────────────────────────┘
```

START Eskdale   **Grid ref.** NY 211011

DISTANCE 5 miles/8km   **ASCENT** 1600ft/487m

ORDNANCE SURVEY MAPS
1:50,000 - Landranger 89 **or** 90   1:25,000 - Outdoor Leisure 6

ACCESS Start from the foot of Hardknott Pass in Eskdale. There is a roadside parking area just above the cattle-grid above Brotherilkeld. Dalegarth (near Boot, 2½ miles) is served by the Ravenglass & Eskdale Railway from Ravenglass, on the Cumbrian Coast railway.

To most Lakeland visitors the name Hard Knott will conjure up visions of the road pass with its hairpin bends and severe gradients, or at best the Roman fort, Mediobogdum, on a shelf on its flanks. The fell of Hard Knott, however, remains a mystery, yet no other fell, great or small, is so well placed for appraising the range of mountains encircling the headwaters of the Esk - England's finest.

S This walk is something of a break from the majority in this book, in that most of the time spent on the fell is away from regular paths. Settled weather is required not only to aid navigation but also to appreciate the mountain panorama. A useful pointer is to only commence the walk if the higher tops are free from cloud, as it would be almost criminal to miss out on their contribution.

From the cattle-grid head up the pass, and when the left-hand wall breaks away, leave the verges of the road in favour of a green path rising up to the left to gain the exciting remains of the Roman fort of Hardknott Castle. Like a castle in the air it guards Eskdale, astride the line of the Roman road between Ambleside and Ravenglass. Looking directly down the valley to the sea, one cannot fail to appreciate the strategic nature of the fort, nor marvel at the Roman efficiency.

After a potter round, head for the north-west gateway overlooking the upper section of Eskdale. Turn right along the outside to the top corner, then head away above a pronounced drop to the valley. At once there are stupendous views across the deep trough to the mighty peaks of the Scafell range, and along with the pyramid of Bowfell to their right, this wild bunch will continue to dominate the scene.

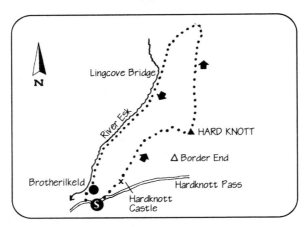

Though never more than sketchy, the path's course is self-evident, rising gently along the grassy shelf above the fall to the left: high to the right, the rock-defended cone of Hard Knott's subsidiary, Border End, repels any attempts at climbing in that direction. Continuing to rise with the imposing face of Yew Crags ahead, the slim path crosses the remains of a wall to rise above the crag. Head on again, virtually level and fading all the time, to the head of a splendid ravine between tall rock walls, a grand moment. Rounding a corner just beyond, all signs of the trod have gone, and ahead slopes of scree tumble to the Esk.

While the river seems a long way below, the freshly revealed chain of crags up to the right seem more distant still. At this point the tower of Eskdale Needle can be discerned by the keen eye, being set in the crags left of centre but not yet appearing detached from them. The aim is to scale the grassy flank between loose rocks and low outcrops to gain the amphitheatre below the crags. The sooner more height is gained the sooner the Needle presents itself, projecting from its crags: when it does, one will wonder how it escaped attention for so long.

With surprising ease one should soon be virtually level with it, and can then simply contour across to the beckoning pinnacle. The isolation of this remarkable block ensures only a handful of visitors ever come to appraise the 50 foot drop on its valley side.

Readily accepting that the scramble to its top is a little too ambitious, pass behind the needle and up onto the knoll behind. From here a conspicuous grass gully rises directly up the final slopes to gain the top of the fell. Escape a small marsh by going left by a line of rocks, after which a rock barrier precedes the final defence, another fringe of rock with the cairn perched defiantly above. Aside from the view's obvious features, a good section of the Duddon Valley reveals itself, from its very beginnings on Wrynose Pass. When the mountainous dalehead of the Esk puts on its Sunday best, this is a first-class place to be, the awesome view being complemented by a rare absence of paths.

Begin the extremely gentle descent by turning north along the broad ridge, being novel in that it declines in towards the mountains, further enhancing the vista across to the high fells. Beyond a steeper grassy drop to a marshy saddle, a thin trod makes the negligible rise along to a small cairn on a final knoll - a superb viewing station. Beyond this all is grass, and ahead the col linking Hard Knott with its parent fell Crinkle Crags above the head of Mosedale is visible, while to the left Cam Spout falls into Great Moss in the lap of the Scafells. The trod leads amiably on down the final section, and when it fades incline slightly left to drop to the distinct path tracing Lingcove Beck.

Turning down to the left a steeper drop soon ensues above the exuberant waters of the beck, where lovely falls are decorated by some hardy rowan. Path and stream quickly descend to the graceful arch of Lingcove Bridge, alongside a sheepfold. As Lingcove Beck joins the Esk, one could easily while away an hour in this delectable corner. Without crossing the bridge our path continues downstream, and within yards the newly charged Esk breaks into tumbling falls and crystal pools: this is truly a walk in heaven. Up to the left meanwhile the dark tower of Eskdale Needle breaks the skyline, while a glance back over the shoulder reveals the classic pyramid of Bowfell.

Beyond a stile the path crosses two rough grazing enclosures to regain the riverbank, which is then accompanied tightly downstream to Brotherilkeld. The farm road bears right to run out onto the main road, just below the cattle-grid at the foot of the pass.

SUMMITS
HARTER FELL   2146ft/654m

START *Eskdale*   **Grid ref.** *NY 211011*

DISTANCE *5½ miles/9km*   **ASCENT** *1900ft/579m*

ORDNANCE SURVEY MAPS
1:50,000 - Landranger 96 and either 89 or 90
1:25,000 - Outdoor Leisure 6

ACCESS *Start from the foot of Hardknott Pass in Eskdale. There is a roadside parking area just above the cattle-grid above Brotherilkeld. Dalegarth (near Boot, 2½ miles) is served by the Ravenglass & Eskdale Railway from Ravenglass, on the Cumbrian Coast railway.*

Harter Fell soars to an inspiring pyramid that forms the backdrop to many a rural scene. Lakeland's most isolated 2000-footer occupies an enviable position looking across upper Eskdale to the country's highest tops.

S Leave the parking area above the cattle-grid at the foot of the pass without setting foot on the road, by taking an inviting little stone-arched bridge over the adjacent Hardknott Gill West. A well made path heads off to the right, steadily at first and then rising more earnestly across the colourful lower slopes of Harter Fell. Though this splendid path barely calls for rest stops, they are certainly required to embrace the rapidly unfolding panorama of Eskdale, from the green valley floor to the mountainous dalehead.

After crossing the charming Dodknott Gill and attendant wall, the craggy summit is glimpsed high to the left. Another splendid surviving section of this old pathway slants up to approach the larger Spothow Gill. Passing through another gate it climbs parallel with the beck to quickly reach a cairn marking a fork.

Appropriately, the summit re-appears at this point, beckoning high to the left. Take the left branch rising as a pleasant grassy way to begin the second section of the ascent. Strengthened by a path climbing from lower down Eskdale, the well trodden route forges more steeply upwards, with craggy ground to the left as the heather zone is entered. Gaining height, the Pillar group reveals itself to the left of the Scafells. This remains a splendid climb all the way to the summit, which finally returns to view just minutes ahead as the going eases. The path bounds eagerly on to gain one of Lakeland's grandest felltops.

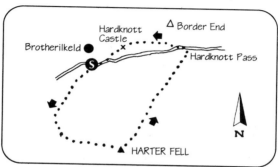

Several upthrusts of pure rock ensure a thrilling conclusion to the ascent, the first, obviously lower one being stood to the right of the path. Other summit features stand to the left, where the highest and finest point is a splendid tor overlooking a humbled Ordnance Survey column: a minor scramble up its east side is required to claim its top. A second tor stands to its east, but is clearly inferior to the main one. If graced with suitable weather conditions the view of the Scafell massif will produce an unforgettable experience, one of the truly great mountain pictures, but don't forget the charms of the Duddon Valley and the indented coastline beyond.

In unfavourable conditions, the best return route is to reverse the ascent, but in clear weather an interesting and varied return can be made by a prolonged descent incorporating Hardknott Pass. This involves first heading east from the summit to escape the rim of cliffs, then striking north-east on a clear path working gently down the broad ridge that eventually leads to the summit of the pass. The thin path can be followed most of the way, keeping well to the right (east) of the true, knobbly crest of the ridge.

This easy angled, grassy descent affords ample time to appraise England's finest mountain line-up. The path crosses a stile on meeting the top edge of the plantation on the Duddon Valley flank, and continues on through some small marshy sections above the afforested darkness. When the trees below end, a stile leads over another fence by a reedy pool. A fainter path runs on through an old wall, then the green course of a bridleway can be picked up to lead left, out onto the road just beneath the summit of the pass.

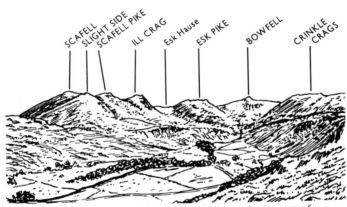

SCAFELL SLIGHT SIDE SCAFELL PIKE ILL CRAG Esk Hause ESK PIKE BOWFELL CRINKLE CRAGS

The mountains of upper Eskdale from the early stages of the ascent, Harter Fell

Turning left on gaining the pass, the motor road can be vacated at the first sharp bend beneath the craggy ramparts of Border End, and a grassy path heads off at a gentler angle than the road. Though a little faint through bracken and marsh, it leads quickly down to the dramatically sited Hardknott Castle. This Roman fort of Mediobogdum sits on a ledge high above the floor of Eskdale, astride the line of the Roman road between Ambleside and Ravenglass.

Looking directly down the valley to the sea, one cannot fail to appreciate the strategic nature of the fort, nor marvel at the Roman efficiency. From the far side of the fort a green path continues down to a wall corner and concludes on the wide verges of the lower zigzags of the pass above Brotherilkeld.

CAW

SUMMITS	
CAW	1735ft/529m
PIKES	1538ft/469m

START Seathwaite

Grid ref. SD 228960

DISTANCE 6 miles/9½km

ASCENT 1600ft/487m

ORDNANCE SURVEY MAPS
1:50,000 - Landranger 96   1:25,000 - Outdoor Leisure 6

ACCESS Start from the centre of this Duddon Valley hamlet. Parking is limited to odd corners by the Newfield Inn, while there is a small layby just past the church. Several other spaces further north are all well placed on the return route. Postbus from Broughton in Furness.

Of the various tops borne out of Dow Crag's south ridge, Caw is by far the most interesting, typically Lakeland in character and tapering to a beautiful pyramid to match Harter Fell across the Duddon. Tucked away from the mainstream of Lakeland fellwalking, Caw shares its delights with only the discerning few. Seen from the Duddon Valley it assumes a classic mountain structure, and suggests an altitude far in excess of its very modest figure.

S From the church head back towards the Newfield Inn, but at the sharp bend just before it take a gate on the left. A stony track known as Park Head Road rises unconvincingly between walls, but through a second gate it turns right with the wall and the route is then obvious. Remaining stony for a while, it rises gently with the wall through a few trees and on up the fellside. At once there are good views back to the pyramid of Harter Fell across the valley, with the greater peaks of Bowfell and Crinkle Crags set further back.

A long quarter mile beyond an intervening gate, a wide green track doubles sharply back to the left. This is the access road to the former Caw Quarry, and maintains the undemanding nature of the ascent.

Ahead now enjoy views to the head of Eskdale, with the nearer Grey Friar and Dow Crag straight in front. This splendidly engineered track expires at the slate workings after a short zigzag up to a ruined hut and a dark, dripping level. By this stage the Scafell group is also largely in place.

Caw's summit is still several hundred feet up the flank behind, but a line of cairns send a very faint path half-right up the slope. As height is gained it becomes less clear, by which stage strike left up the easy slopes to conclude in style. The Ordnance Survey column appears well before it is gained, and a modest path forms for the final expectant minutes.

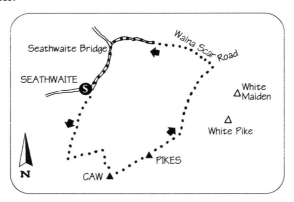

The column is cemented onto a rock ridge that forms the summit, and with the ground falling away on all sides this is a supreme vantage point. On a clear day pride of place goes to the Scafell line-up around the head of Eskdale, though the length of the Duddon Valley is rarely seen in such detail, backed by Harter Fell, the Black Combe ridge and great sweeps of the coastline - including the Duddon's own estuary.

To the north-east the bulk of the nearby Coniston massif keep a watchful eye behind the craggy wall of White Pike, its nearest top. This is also the direction to take, heading down to the minor depression across which the rocky little top of Pikes is more than prominent. Keeping left of rough ground, a thin trod can be traced all the way down to the tilted saddle, and even more faintly up the five minute pull onto Pikes' cheerful little top.

From Pikes a similar line should be taken towards the aggressive looking White Pike, though the fading trod will be unlikely to be traced for long. Drop gently right to the outflow of the main, marshy depression of Yaud Mire, where a green track will be found running along its far side. Rise gently left on this old way, which encounters some moist moments as it rises to the far end of the saddle. Here it gains the Duddon flank of the ridge, and suddenly transforms into a delightful green way.

The former Walna Scar Quarries are just ahead now, and the track contours along to the extensive spoil heaps. Beyond the spoil heaps and ruined buildings the track continues above a wall, and on past an isolated spoil heap to meet the broad Walna Scar track at a gate. A gate just before that last spoil heap suggests a handy short-cut on an old green way slanting down to the main track.

Turn down the track for an uncomplicated and speedy return to the valley, with the adjacent Long House Gill offering several attractive falls. Nearer the dale floor the way becomes surfaced as the access road from Seathwaite Tarn joins in, and keeping left at a minor junction the valley road is met just above Seathwaite Bridge. Bear left on this quiet road back down to Seathwaite, in the delightful company not of the Duddon itself, but the effervescent Tarn Beck.

Looking back to Caw from Pikes

SUMMITS
STOUPDALE HEAD   1548ft/472m
BLACK COMBE   1968ft/600m

START *Beckside*   **Grid ref.** *SD 152847*

DISTANCE *6½ miles/10½km*   **ASCENT** *1985ft/605m*

ORDNANCE SURVEY MAPS
1:50,000 - Landranger 96   1:25,000 - Outdoor Leisure 6

ACCESS Start from Beckside, north of Millom on the A595 between Silecroft and Hallthwaites. There is a roadside parking area opposite the entrance to the Whitecombe Valley. Railways stations and bus services at Silecroft and The Green, 2½ miles away.

A circuit of the lovely Whitecombe Valley, linking modest White Combe with the famous landmark of Black Combe. Incredible coastal views offer a walk with a difference, and many first-time visitors will be surprised to discover this unfrequented country is just as much in the National Park as Keswick and Ambleside!

S Head east along the road for just a minute up the hill, then escape at a stile on the right. Head away with the hedge, and at the corner a track drops down through a gate. Bear left on this, merging with another and heading back out to the road. Just before it bends to a gate onto the road opposite Fox and Goose Cottages, a line of hawthorns point straight ahead to a stile onto the road. Just 10 yards to the left take a leafy byway. Though initially poorly drained, it quickly improves as it heads away. At a wall corner a gate gives access onto a corner of the open fell, and a few yards up to the left a pronounced groove begins, slanting half-right through the bracken. Immediately there are extensive views, looking over the Duddon Estuary to the Furness heights, with Kirkby Moor windfarm prominent; on a clear day the Howgill Fells and Ingleborough can be discerned much further.

A green path runs along the parapet of the sunken way: keep to the higher left branch at a fork, though both meet to continue up as one. As a corner is rounded the Coniston Fells appear ahead, as more of Lakeland steadily appears. The path fades as it swings up to the left out of the bracken and onto a plateau. White Combe's upper slopes are now brought into play, but this moment is dominated by the sudden presence of Black Combe to the west, displaying its splendid scooped combe of tumbling screes and vegetated crags. Back on our present ridge, the shapely knolls of White Hall Knott to the left offer a worthwhile stroll to incorporate them at little cost, and are blest with fine views across the Whitecombe Valley.

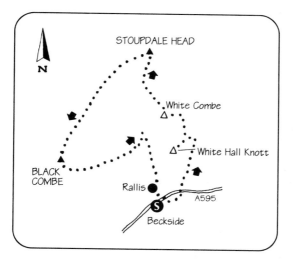

On the plateau, meanwhile, the base of White Combe's upper slope sees two re-emerging grooves raking up the bilberry flank. As the upper one becomes reed-choked a simple little pull up to the left leads to the wind shelter and great sprawl of stones on White Combe. Though this is sometimes described as a separate fell, there is no discernible re-ascent from the ridge to which it belongs, so it is better to concentrate on the new features of the view. The Coniston Fells have now been joined by the Lakeland giants, with Scafell, Scafell Pike, Ill Crag, Esk Pike, Bowfell and Crinkle Crags arrayed from left to right - Harter Fell also appears with distinction.

The walk resumes by tramping the continuing ridge north towards the main ridge at Stoupdale Head. Everywhere broad and grassy, a slim path leads along to a clump of reeds, then slowly falters. If desperate to push on to Black Combe, simply trend left to the col at Whitecombe Head, where an old drove road rising from Whitecombe Beck is met (this also offers an easy, very clear descent route). Otherwise, forge on up the gentle slope in front to gain the plateau-like top of Stoupdale Head (not named as such on OS maps). A tiny cairn stands rather forlorn, but offers a good view north to Buck Barrow and Whit Fell, while more distantly Kirk Fell and Great Gable have sneaked in to the left of Scafell.

Leave by heading south-west towards Black Combe, reaching Whitecombe Head at a reedy patch. At this point the path continuing from the drove road is met, so turn right on it to circle the rim and begin a prolonged, exceptionally easy climb onto Black Combe's summit. Towards the top the rim of Blackcombe Screes comes within yards on the left, and is worth a detour in good weather to survey the awesome prospect of this shattered slate wall. Impressive as this is, it must be conceded the map is over generous with its craggy claims. For the summit, cut back to the main path which fades just short of the highest point.

The summit is an extensive plateau, in the centre of which an Ordnance Survey column is ringed by a large, crumbling stone shelter. Much has been written about the panorama, and no less a source than Wordsworth has had his say. The aspect of mountain Lakeland, grand as it is, fills only a small portion of the whole, and more time is likely to be spent taking advantage of the vast seascape on offer. Close to hand is the Duddon Estuary and the rolling foothills of southern Lakeland, while clearer days will have one scouring the horizons for the Isle of Man, Scotland, and even Ireland and Wales. These are not always in evidence - Snowdon, for example, is almost twice the distance of Snaefell, on the Isle of Man!

Despite its modest altitude, Black Combe is one of Lakeland's major fells. The fact that it is many long miles to the next higher ground, coupled with its position overlooking many miles of coastline makes Black Combe an important eminence, the overlord of South Cumberland. The massive moorland ridge of which Black Combe is the terminus stands almost island-like between the valley of the Duddon and the formidable barrier of the Irish Sea. Only a slender strip of land keeps the waters from the base of Black Combe, negotiated by important road and rail links to West Cumberland from the town of Millom, over which Black Combe keeps a watchful eye.

Leave by heading south for 200 yards to a small tarn, then swing left (east) to quickly encounter the rim of the combe again. With the cragginess fading, simply aim straight down this broad shoulder of the fell. As the going steepens, incredibly extensive bilberry slopes take over, and this vegetation offers a useful cushion for the feet. As a reedy sidestream forms, keep left of it to descend to Blackcombe Beck. Cross the main beck just above the confluence, where there is little bracken to hamper progress.

Use a sheep trod slanting back out to rise onto a broad green way. Turn down this splendid droveway which quickly angles back left to drop into the main valley of Whitecombe Beck, where it meets the green valley track. Turn right down this, quickly passing above a dark mine entrance and spoilheap of old copper workings. The green track and its lovely surroundings offer a charming finish in the company of the little stream. At the intake wall the track goes through a gate to run above the beck and its little wood to emerge at the idyllic corner of the former Whicham Mill. Its drive leads out through Rallis Farm exactly back to the starting point.

White Combe and the Duddon Estuary from Black Combe Screes

TABLE OF SUMMITS

	FELL	FEET	METRES	
1	SCAFELL PIKE **M**	3209	978	....
2	SCAFELL	3163	964	....
3	Symond's Knott #•	3146	959	....
4	ILL CRAG •	3068	935	....
5	BROAD CRAG •	3064	934	....
6	GREAT END	2986	910	....
7	GREAT GABLE **M**	2949	899	....
8	PILLAR **M**	2926	892	....
9	GRASMOOR **M**	2795	852	....
10	SCOAT FELL	2759	841	....
11	EEL CRAG	2753	839	....
12	RED PIKE (Wasdale)	2710	826	....
13	Steeple #	2687	819	....
14	HIGH STILE **M**	2648	807	....
15	LINGMELL	2648	807	....
16	KIRK FELL **M**	2631	802	....
17	HAYCOCK	2615	797	....
18	KIRK FELL EAST TOP •	2582	787	....
19	SAIL	2536	773	....
20	WANDOPE	2533	772	....
21	HOPEGILL HEAD	2526	770	....
22	Slight Side #	2499	762	....
23	RED PIKE (Buttermere)	2477	755	....
24	WHITESIDE	2359	719	....
25	Ladyside Pike #•	2306	703	....
26	WHITELESS PIKE	2165	660	....
27	HARTER FELL **M**	2146	654	....
28	FLEETWITH PIKE	2126	648	....
29	Honister Crag #•	2077	633	....
30	Looking Stead #•	2057	627	....
31	YEWBARROW	2057	627	....
32	STIRRUP CRAG •	2021	616	....
33	Illgill Head **M**	1998	609	....
34	Black Combe **M** •	1968	600	....
35	Haystacks	1958	597	....
36	Middle Fell	1909	582	....
37	Blake Fell **M**	1880	573	....
38	Hard Knott **M**	1801	549	....
39	Carling Knott •	1784	544	....
40	Whin Rigg	1755	535	....
41	Caw •	1735	529	....
42	Gavel Fell	1726	526	....
43	Crag Fell	1715	523	....
44	Mellbreak **M**	1679	512	....
45	Mellbreak North Top •	1670	509	....
46	Stoupdale Head •	1548	472	....
47	Pikes •	1538	469	....
48	Rannerdale Knotts	1165	355	....

KEY

For walkers who like their hills to be classified:
UPPER CASE - 2000ft fells with at least 100ft/30m of re-ascent ('HEWITT')
\# - minor 2000ft fells   • - non 'WAINWRIGHT' fells
M - fells with at least 500ft/150m of re-ascent ('MARILYN')

INDEX
Summits and other principle features
Walk number refers; Start points in bold

LOG OF THE WALKS

WALK	DATE	NOTES
1		
2		
3		
4		
5		
6		
7		
8		
9		
10		
11		
12		
13		
14		
15		
16		
17		
18		
19		
20		
21		
22		
23		
24		
25		